ukrainian canadians

a survey
of their portrayal
in English-language
works

ukrainian canadians

a survey
of their portrayal
in English-language
works

by Frances Swyripa

Published **The**
for the Canadian **University**
Institute of **of Alberta**
Ukrainian Studies by **Press**

1978

Published for
The Canadian Institute of Ukrainian Studies
by
The University of Alberta Press

Edmonton, Alberta, Canada
1978

Canadian Cataloguing in Publication Data

Swyripa, Frances, 1951-
Ukrainian Canadians

Bibliography: p.
Includes index.
ISBN 0-88864-050-1 bd.
ISBN 0-88864-022-6 pa.

1. Ukrainians in Canada—Historiography.

I. Title
FC106.U5S99   971'.004'91791   C78-002012-X

Cover design: J. Frascara

Printed by Printing Services of
The University of Alberta

The Alberta Library in Ukrainian-Canadian Studies
A series of original works and reprints relating to Ukrainians in
Canada, issued under the editorial supervision of the Canadian
Institute of Ukrainian Studies, University of Alberta, Edmonton

Contents

Notes

Preface

The object of this study was to examine those works in the English language relevant to the history of Ukrainians in Canada, determining the areas of concentration, dominant themes, and developing perspectives that characterize this literature. A chronological approach seemed to illustrate best the growing sophistication of Ukrainian-Canadian historiography as it has progressed from the initially superficial descriptions of Ukrainian pioneers by ill-informed Anglo-Saxon observers to the more thorough research into Ukrainian-Canadian history by serious students of the subject. The survey was restricted to English-language sources because of their accessibility to large numbers of people.

With research, it became apparent that the major contributions to the literature on Ukrainians in Canada reflected an evolving concept of the role, contribution, and status of Ukrainian Canadians against the background of changing views of Canada's national identity. For this reason the study has been organized according to the major periods in the development of Canadian consciousness: from the original emphasis on Anglo-conformity through the continuation of assimilative pressures and the germination of a mosaic concept during the transitional inter-war years, to the recent acceptance of a multicultural expression of Canadian identity.

These developments in consciousness reflect the impact of daily life in an evolving Canadian environment and the influence of the varying nature of each wave of immigrants: the agricultural character of the pre-World War I pioneers, the nationally-conscious colouring of the inter-war immigrants, and the influx of displaced persons after 1945. Works have been grouped generically within these divisions but are discussed individually as to thesis, orientation, and content. The present work concludes with a bibliography of consulted sources, supplemented with biographical sketches of authors (when such information was available) and a note on existing Ukrainian-Canadian bibliographies.

Viewed collectively, English-language literature on Ukrainian Canadians not only records the history of one of the most dynamic ethnic groups in Canada but also reflects the evolution in thought regarding the value of contributions by non-British and non-French segments of the Canadian population.

The suggestions and encouragement offered by Dr. Ivan L. Rudnytsky, Dr. Lewis H. Thomas and Dr. Manoly R. Lupul, are gratefully acknowledged. I would also like to thank St. John's Institute in Edmonton for the Samuel F. Woloshyn Memorial Summer Award which I received in 1973. Its support during the initial stages of research was most helpful.

Introduction

Ukrainians being one of the more visible and vocal ethnic
minority groups in Canada, it is noteworthy that the literature
about them has consistently reflected current interpretations of
Canadian identity and destiny as they took into account the so-
called "Third Force." Ukrainian-Canadian historiography exists
today as a legitimate and accepted discipline in both the
Ukrainian and English languages simply because the circumstances of Canadian nationhood have forced the recognition
of ethnic diversity. In particular, the English-language literature
on Ukrainians in Canada, when examined chronologically and
according to the distinct phases in the growth of Canadian
national consciousness, aptly demonstrates the progress towards
eventual acceptance of the concept of diversity. The present study
is a survey of this literature.[1] It hopes to establish Ukrainian-
Canadian historiography in the English language as a branch of
general Canadian historical scholarship which evolved from
amateur and superficial commentary on Ukrainian-Canadian life
through systematic research in specialized areas to the synthesis
of all spheres of Ukrainian-Canadian development.

As the quantity of English-language literature on Ukrainians in
Canada is limited, a relatively extensive survey of existing
material is feasible, although practical concerns and the diversity
of sources demand discrimination. With minor exceptions, only
published works — be they scholarly monographs or more
popular studies — and theses written in Canada to 1970 have been
selected for examination. Newspapers have been excluded as a
survey of newspaper opinion would constitute a study in itself and
similar views can be obtained elsewhere. Scholarly articles have
received comprehensive treatment while those of a more popular
nature have been consulted at random, since a great proportion of
this literature is of a trivial or repetitive character. Similarly,
government papers and reports and unpublished manuscripts

have received only marginal attention. Although arbitrary, these restrictions do not detract from the usefulness of a survey.

The mass Ukrainian immigration to Canada, to be abruptly terminated by the outbreak of war in 1914, was a movement of peasant agriculturists who were conservative in outlook, mostly illiterate, attached to the soil, and who were alienated culturally, linguistically, and religiously from the rest of Canadian society. To maintain the British character of Canada and to ensure its continued primacy, Canadian institutions vigorously campaigned to imbue Ukrainian immigrants with an appreciation of British-Canadian ideals and institutions. Anglo-Saxon writers frequently studied Ukrainian settlers — the most conspicuous and foreign of the "New Canadians" — for their adaptability to British-Canadian norms and standards. Motivated by a concern for Canadian national progress, these writers did not see Ukrainians as a legitimate collectivity in themselves, and reveal little of value to an understanding of the historical development of Ukrainian community life in Canada.

In the inter-war period, weakening imperial ties compelled British Canada to resist absorption into an homogeneous American society, and with the resumption of large-scale immigration the question of the "ideal" immigrant once again became crucial. Writers appraised the worth of Ukrainian Canadians by considering their physical role in the building of the nation, by measuring their adaptability with racial statistics for mental illness and crime, and by assessing the degree of assimilation in their community outlook and national consciousness. On the other hand, there emerged individuals who tolerated a certain amount of diversity and were willing to concede that not only did tradition ease adjustment but that loyalty to those things Ukrainian and a desire for Ukrainian independence were not necessarily un- or anti-Canadian. Variety acquired value in some of the commentary on identity. The co-existence of two trends — assimilation and the "mosaic" — in the literature of the inter-war years characterizes the time as a transitional period since a clear idea of the Ukrainian's role as a Canadian had not yet crystallized.

Although Anglo-Saxons continued to write on the Ukrainian Canadians during World War II, primarily motivated by their dedication to the Allied war effort, succeeding years witnessed their eclipse by Ukrainian-Canadian writers. The question of assimilation did not vanish, but the emphasis shifted. The

Ukrainians refined the "mosaic" concept to stress their integration into Canadian political, economic, and social life while retaining their historical and cultural heritage within a Ukrainian-Canadian collectivity. With the bilingual and bicultural debate in Canada during the 1960s came a re-examination of the place and role of non-British and non-French groups in the population. By 1971 Canadian identity had been redefined in terms of multiculturalism within a bilingual framework. Studies of Ukrainian Canadians during this period reflected the controversy still surrounding the issue, as Ukrainian writers in particular continued to portray the duality of their Canadian identity.

Unlike literature in the Ukrainian language, English-language works on Ukrainians in Canada were initially detached from the embryonic Ukrainian-Canadian community. Nevertheless, by their very accessibility to a mass national audience, they enjoy a scope and influence unknown to Ukrainian-language works, confined as they are to a select audience by the barrier of language. If integration continues to divest Ukrainian Canadians of their language, it is likely that Ukrainian publications will be reduced to a minor and academic role in Ukrainian-Canadian life, with corresponding gains to Ukrainian-Canadian historiography in English.

The Period of
Acquaintanceship*

As initial references to Ukrainians[1] were sporadic, one must
examine a wide range of sources to obtain an accurate indication
of the contemporary understanding of the newly-arrived
Ukrainian immigrants. Much of the literature contains casual
allusions to or descriptions of the strange and colourful
Ukrainian as encountered by the Anglo-Saxon. For this reason,
incidental comments acquire a significance subsequently lost
through repetition and submersion by serious studies on
Ukrainian Canadians. The bulk of the material on Ukrainians in
Canada prior to World War I was written by government
officials, educationalists, and missionaries, as the state, the
school, and Canadian religious organizations experienced first
prolonged contact with Ukrainian settlers. Their concern for the
British character of Canada and her national prosperity —
evident in their immediate and aggressive interest in Ukrainians
— was corroborated by the tenor of the literature of those years.
Although research was in its infancy, much of the literature
produced served later students of Ukrainian-Canadian history as
primary source material on this earliest phase of Ukrainian life in
Canada.

The annual reports of the Department of the Interior and the
Departments of Education in Manitoba, Saskatchewan, and
Alberta constituted the first consistent public sources of
information on Ukrainians. Intended to outline the implementation of policy, problems, and progress, they were largely factual
and unimaginative annual statements of activities and
developments. They concentrated on the administrative details
related to immigration and the settlement of land, and on the

---

*For stylistic purposes, only the author, abbreviated title, and date of a specific work
appear in the text of the study. Bibliographic data and biographical information
outlining the qualifications and associations with the Ukrainian-Canadian community
of several authors are contained in the bibliography.

establishment of "proper" schools in Ukrainian districts.

The majority of the Department of the Interior reports focused on practical considerations facing the government agencies that had to deal with peasant immigrants. They were little interested in the background or nature of the Ukrainian peasant beyond the occasional observation that he seemed thrifty, industrious, eager to learn, and likely to be a successful farmer. However, the Department of the Interior was not totally oblivious to the need for Canada to become acquainted with the homeland and traditional lifestyle of her colonists. W.T.R. Preston, Inspector of European Agencies for the Department of the Interior, journeyed to Galicia in 1899 solely to inquire into the manner of life of Galician-Ukrainian peasants in their native surroundings. His description of peasant village life and land use in eastern Galicia was contained in the report submitted to his Department in 1899. The picture created was positive and Preston concluded his report optimistically:

> I am fully aware that the Galician whom I have seen here, neat and tidy in his attire, although somewhat quaint to the Anglo-Saxon eyes, cheerful in his demeanor, and deferential to a marked degree, does not bear a strong resemblance to the Galician whom I have seen arrive in Canada, haggard and tired after four weeks' travel by land and sea. But I have seen his home, the village whence he has come, the farm land that he has cultivated, and I have had no difficulty in arriving at the conclusion that, given a chance in our country, amid its free institutions, he will quickly become Anglicized, and, through his natural thrift and industry, will develop in a few years into a citizen of whom the most sensitive Canadian will not be ashamed.[2]

Preston's findings were in sharp contrast to statements by many later writers who complained that a lack of hygiene, general untidiness and overcrowding, a plain and unappetizing diet, and the presence of animals close to or in the house did not reflect the stresses of pioneer life but were typical of conditions in Galicia and inherent in the Ukrainian way of life.

The reports issued by the Department of Education in the three prairie provinces specifically discussed the problems raised in conjunction with the expressed desire of the Ukrainian settlers for education in the Ukrainian language. Privately, Canadian educationalists and teachers also were investigating the introduction of the public school into foreign settlement blocs and the teaching of the English language, British ideals, and Canadian ways to the Ukrainian. The writings of individual teachers generally provided more personal accounts of education in the Ukrainian blocs as well as descriptions of the Ukrainians and their way of life.[3] Literature on the role of the public school in assimilating Ukrainian immigrants to British-Canadian ideals and standards continued to appear well into the inter-war period as studies assessed the programs and progress in this field.

Whereas the Canadian Protestant churches, notably the Methodist and Presbyterian denominations, were motivated by missionary zeal to carry evangelical Christianity to Ukrainians in the conviction that an authoritarian church and ritualistic religion were evil, the Roman Catholic Church laboured to save the leaderless Ukrainian Greek Catholics for Rome. As Roman Catholic activity among Ukrainians was conducted primarily by French and Belgian missionaries, much of the resultant literature appeared in French or Flemish, and therefore has contributed to the development of Ukrainian-Canadian historiography outside the English- and Ukrainian-speaking communities.[4] Although resented by Ukrainians as a traditional instrument of Polonization, the Roman Catholic Church was less alien to Ukrainian historical experience than was Canadian Protestantism. Roman Catholic writings showed greater comprehension of Ukrainian religious history in Uniatism and Orthodoxy than did those by Anglo-Saxon Protestants, who produced considerable confusion in attempting to clarify the religious divisions in Ukrainian society. Propelled overwhelmingly by religious principles and governed by the international spirit of Catholicism, the Roman Catholic Church did not reveal the same patriotic commitment as did the Methodist and Presbyterian churches to Canadianizing Ukrainians in the British mould.[5]

To the two major Canadian Protestant churches, the value and truth of evangelical Christianity became equated with the notion of the superiority of British-Canadian ideals, institutions, and way of life.[6] Adopting the motto "Canada for Christ," the Methodists and Presbyterians understood their mission to be not simply the evangelization of Ukrainians for their own sakes, but also their evangelization and assimilation in the interests of Canada.[7] Their religious journals and official reports of various developments in the Ukrainian mission field repeatedly

3

emphasized the necessity of both evangelization and assimilation to protect the nation from the false religion and questionable level of civilization introduced by the Ukrainian peasant.[8] Although Presbyterian and Methodist missions among Ukrainians ultimately vanished under the United Church of Canada, those involved in this effort to educate Ukrainians in Protestantism and British-Canadian democracy have left different accounts of their experiences.

A perhaps unanticipated development resulted from Protestant missionary contact with the Ukrainian settlers. Notwithstanding the fact that the Anglo-Saxon in Canada encountered mainly Ukrainian peasant culture, ignorance of the Ukrainian historical and literary heritage did not remain universal. Among the Protestant clergy serving Ukrainians were those who became academically interested in Ukrainian history and literature and undertook serious study of the Ukrainian language. In later years they contributed to the growth of Ukrainian studies proper in North America. A limited but early contribution was made by the Reverend Dr. Alexander J. Hunter, a Presbyterian medical missionary among Ukrainians at Teulon, Manitoba, for a quarter century. In 1922 he published *The Kobzar of the Ukraine,*[9] an annotated translation of selected poetry by Taras Shevchenko. Another Presbyterian clergyman also working among the Manitoban Ukrainians, the Reverend Percival Cundy, engaged in more sustained and scholarly Ukrainian literary pursuits. Acquiring an excellent command of Ukrainian, he achieved considerable repute as a translator and literary critic of Ukrainian works, particularly those of the West Ukrainian writer, Ivan Franko, and the East Ukrainian poetess, Lesya Ukrayinka.[10] Marko Vovchok, Mykhaylo Kotsiubinsky, and Vasyl Stefanyk were other Ukrainian literary figures of interest to Cundy. Cundy and Hunter were unquestionably atypical of the Protestant missionaries among Ukrainians, but their admiration for Ukrainian literature marked the beginning of the transmission of Ukrainian culture to Anglo-Saxons, although on a limited scale.

By the close of World War I, government and Protestant church interest in Ukrainians had declined. The mass Ukrainian immigration had been halted and was to resume on a much-diminished scale after the war; hence, Ukrainian immigrants were no longer a major concern to federal government departments, and mention of them accordingly dwindled. In 1916 the bilingual school clause was repealed in Manitoba and with growing

Ukrainian acceptance of English-language instruction in all three prairie provinces, the progress of education in Ukrainian districts was no longer noted in the annual reports issued by the Departments of Education. The consolidation of the Ukrainian community around its traditional churches, with the establishment of the Greek Catholic hierarchy in 1913 and the formation of the Ukrainian Greek Orthodox Church of Canada in 1918, forced the Presbyterians and Methodists to admit the failure of their drive to convert the Ukrainians to Protestantism. Ukrainians then disappeared as a subject of concern in Protestant publications, which later tended to dismiss the Ukrainian experiment as a passing phase.[11] Lastly, during the war the term "New Canadian" came to replace "Foreigner" as the authorized designation of the non-British immigrant, signifying that as assimilation or adaptation proceeded, however slowly, Anglo-Canadian attitudes changed towards their new fellow citizens.

The study of Ukrainians through World War I continued to be the almost exclusive domain of government departments, educationalists, and churches, but a fourth category also produced some literature. Those who had only marginal contact with Ukrainians and their colonies often described the unusual and the picturesque to an audience unfamiliar with the peasants of eastern Europe. Their comments remained cursory, consisting largely of observations limited to prominent features — clothing, church and cottage architecture, food, living conditions, customs, and religious observances.

Much of the failure to understand Ukrainians as members of a national collectivity resulted from the fact that at the time of their arrival in Canada they had long been stateless and were physically divided between two empires. They came not as citizens of a Ukrainian state but as subjects of Austria-Hungary and Russia. The peasants themselves were able to convey little of Ukrainian national history to inquisitive Anglo-Saxons or to clarify but slightly the various nuances of Galician, Bukovinian, Austrian, Ruthenian, Little Russian, and other appellations that they received in Canada. The term "Ukrainian," while steadily gaining popularity among Austrian and Russian Ukrainians before World War I, was used irregularly by them in Canada until the events of the Ukrainian Revolution and the existence of an independent Ukraine from 1917 to 1921 elevated their national consciousness.

In 1906 Michael A. Sherbinin, a Russian graduate of St.

Frances Swyripa

Petersburg University and an instructor of Galician youth at Manitoba College, presented a paper to the Historical and Scientific Society of Manitoba entitled "The Galicians Dwelling in Canada and their Origin." Although potentially significant in introducing Anglo-Canada to Ukrainian history, Sherbinin's address failed to fulfill its possibilities. Covering in twelve pages Ukrainian development from prehistoric times to the contemporary situation, with emphasis on the medieval period, the work was hopelessly deficient. What value it did possess was minimized by the fact that the *Transactions of the Historical and Scientific Society of Manitoba* were restricted to an exclusive audience with little influence beyond academic circles. It is, nonetheless, worth noting that the Society would have welcomed a paper on Galicians at that early date.

That considerable confusion existed among Canadians as to the identity of the Ukrainian immigrants is evident from the numerous writers who endeavoured to explain their origins ethnically and nationally as a Slavic group. Perhaps the most fantastic array of associations made in an attempt to place the Galicians in their proper niche in European civilization is the following statement by someone sympathetic towards Ukrainian immigration:

> As we drive west and north-west [of Saskatoon], we find ourselves among folk who know no English. "Galicians," or "Galatians," they are commonly called. Some of them come from Galicia in the Austrian Empire, but others are Ruthenians or Ukrainians from South-western Russia, and many from Poland, too. They belong, like the Servs and Croats and Montenegrins, the Czechs and Slovaks, and nearly all the Russians, to the great Slavic Race.
>
> But who are the Slavs? Just a branch of the same white race that we ourselves belong to. Their ancestors, like ours, poured through Europe in waves of barbaric invasion from some far eastern home, but settled in Russia and neighbouring lands as our forefathers had passed on to settle on the shores of the Atlantic. The very name "Galician" reminds us of the real kinship between the Galicians of Austria-Hungary, the Galatians of Asia Minor to whom St. Paul wrote his epistle, the inhabitants of France whom Julius Caesar describes as Gauls, and the Celtic Gaels of the British Isles.
>
> Long separated from us they have come to join us again.[12]

6

On the other hand, a feature article on Ruthenians published in the *Winnipeg Free Press* in 1903 clearly outlined the Polish-Ruthenian racial and political tensions in the Austrian province of Galicia and alluded to the Ukrainian national past, proving that certain sectors of Canadian society recognized the factors affecting Ukrainian historical development.[13] In 1921 "Ukrainian" first appeared as an ethnic origin on the Canadian census lists. Eventually, as it came to be the term preferred by Ukrainians in Canada and the different implications in the former names were better understood, interest in nomenclature declined in Anglo-Saxon writings. Initial confusion and inconsistency, however, led to the inaccuracies and vagueness of Ukrainian immigration statistics prior to World War I.

Of the works by those having only marginal contact with the Ukrainians, travel diaries in particular contain interesting vignettes of features of Ukrainian life from the turn of the century to the mid-1920s.[14] Several of the travellers were British or Canadian journalists who journeyed through Canada for either personal or business reasons and recorded their impressions and observations. These men and women constantly sought examples of the peculiar and the quaint to capture the attention of the public at home, and the Galician settlers in their sheepskin coats and headshawls, glimpsed in passage or in their daily routine, furnished ample subject matter. For this reason, the visual features and pronounced or common characteristics of Ukrainians and their colonies were usually highlighted.

As the travellers also wished to determine the future direction of Canada as a nation and component of the British Empire, their comments included judgments of Galicians as prospective Canadians, again from an extremely limited acquaintance. Regardless of the problem they posed for assimilating agencies, the foreigners were recognized as valuable labourers and agriculturists. Already, however, caution was expressed at the establishment of ethnic blocs which hindered assimilation to Canadian norms, although the travellers mentioned little overt resistance to assimilation and even noted that many Galicians seemed to desire it. Simultaneously, concern for the security of the British element in Canada was manifest. As one might expect, the question of the suitability and promise of Ukrainians as Canadian citizens was studied in greater depth by writers having more protracted contact with them.

In 1899, what is perhaps the earliest article on Ukrainian

immigrants — "A Galician Wedding" by Basil C. d'Easum —
appeared in *Canadian Magazine*. It concerned a scheming and
callous Galician peasant in Alberta, recently widowed, who
solicited the services of an Anglican priest to marry a new wife
obtained sight unseen. Both Nikolai Szcheswa Pschitzchisoffsni
— his name undoubtedly deliberately concocted to illustrate his
"foreignness" — and his bride were portrayed as dirty and
slovenly, while at the conclusion of the marriage ceremony,
Nikolai was shown begging fifty cents from the preacher and
stealing his pipe. A caustic remonstrance against the immigration
policies of the Liberal government, d'Easum's article painted the
Galician as a completely negative figure loath to assimilate and
detrimental to Canadian health. Of the literature examining the
Ukrainian peasant of the pre-World War I immigration, few
works revealed the degree of racial prejudice and animosity
contained in "A Galician Wedding."[15]

In 1909 *Canadian Magazine* carried a second article on
Ukrainians. "Winnipeg: The Melting Pot" by George F.
Chipman, a school teacher who taught for some years among
different nationalities in rural Alberta, also expressed reservations as to the desirability of Ukrainian immigration, but
without the hatred and moral indignation that characterized
d'Easum's article. Largely through the Galicians in Winnipeg,
Chipman outlined the problems created for immigrant groups
and Canadian civic and religious authorities by the concentration
of large numbers of foreign immigrants in urban enclaves where
the ways of life, attitudes, and entire orientation were divorced
from the fundamental Anglo-Saxon structure of the city.
Recognizing the chasm separating the Galician from his
accustomed life and the environment into which he was now
thrust, Chipman could appreciate the pressures on the immigrant
in adjusting to his changed condition, new ideas, and institutions.
He also deplored the accompanying tendency for crime and
delinquency and the fertile soil for political corruption by both
Canadians and fellow Galicians. Voicing a theme to be advocated
by all assimilationists and particularly educationalists, Chipman
concluded that while the older generation could only be aided,
pitied, and endured, it was the younger generation that was to be
fostered, watched, and developed into Canadians.

J.H. Hardy, another school teacher among the Albertan
Ukrainians, published a short article in 1913 entitled "The
Ruthenians in Alberta." As the following passage illustrates, his

description of Ruthenians and their living conditions was highly derogatory:

On approaching one of the dwellings one is in dire danger of being torn to pieces by a pack of wolfish, hungry-looking dogs. Should he escape these and open the door, several chickens start out noisily under his feet, and he beholds an old hen and her brood nestling under the stove. In another corner a turkey is mothering her brood, and a family of kittens are playing on the bed: three or four unkempt, dirty urchins cling to their mother's skirts and gaze curiously at the newcomer. The whole establishment reeks with a strong, peculiar Russian [?] odor. If it is about their meal time, the home-made table is freighted with an unlimited supply of boiled eggs, some brown rye or barley bread and a copious supply of murky tea. The most noticeable feature of the dwelling is the lack of cleanliness everywhere in evidence.[16]

Hardy's comments are interesting, particularly when compared to the observations made by W.T.R. Preston during his tour of Galicia. Although the latter's favourable views were perhaps influenced by his position as a civil servant, in his report to the Department of the Interior Preston had explicitly stated that no animal sheds were found attached to houses.[17] Hardy also characterized Ruthenians as avaricious towards each other, liars to a greater or lesser degree, unwilling to honour debts, and too fond of alcohol. Although ostensibly speaking from personal experience, some of his statements were absurd. He asserted that Ruthenian incapacity for mathematics was illustrated by the fact that they elected to detour their roads around sloughs rather than to build through them. Other erroneous statements uttered with equal authority labelled a dish of garlic "sauerkraut" and declared that the Orthodox Church recognized the pope while the Greek Catholic did not. Hardy concluded his brief account by emphasizing the patriotic duty of Anglo-Saxon teachers in educating Ruthenians to Canadian standards; his article was possibly an attempt to enlist readers as teachers or active participants in the Canadianization of Ruthenians.

Ukrainian religious practices also attracted the attention of Anglo-Saxon writers. "Janey Canuck," wife of a Protestant minister and later an Alberta judge, attended a Greek Catholic mass in Mundare, Alberta, and recorded her impressions in

9

"Communing with Ruthenians." Describing the ritual of the Finding of the Holy Cross, she conveyed her own emotional response of awe and reverence for the intense religious passion and devotion of Ukrainians and the pageantry of their worship, although she understood neither. From an acquaintance with Ukrainians in the vicinity of Lamont, Alberta, Miriam Elston provided another description of a Ukrainian mass, but "A Greek Easter Service" was primarily concerned with furnishing a factual, albeit colourful, account of the Greek Orthodox Easter service to an audience unfamiliar with the Eastern rite. Similarly, in "A Ruthenian Day of Days" she gave a graphic report of the consecration of a Greek Orthodox church. Neither Janey Canuck nor Miriam Elston censured Ukrainian religious practices and beliefs, expressing rather a feeling of admiration.

A noted journalist, Elston produced numerous articles on the Ukrainian colony east of Edmonton where she taught in the years prior to World War I. Published in both Canadian and British magazines, they were illustrated with excellent pictures of native costumes, churches, and thatched and plastered dwellings. Some were purely expository attempts to acquaint her Anglo-Canadian readers with the traditions of the people among whom she found herself.[18] Others were more seriously oriented and considered the adaptation of Ukrainians to Canadian life, especially through the efforts of the church, school, and other institutions active in the Ukrainian bloc in Alberta. Although generally sympathetic and understanding in her analysis of Ukrainians and her assessment of their progress, Elston referred to the Ukrainians east of Edmonton interchangeably as Ruthenians and Russians, clearly not grasping the fact that the two constituted distinct and historically antagonistic nationalities.[19]

In her more purposive articles, Elston concentrated on medical activity and enlightenment, and on the education of Ukrainians as undertaken by the Alberta government. The first area of concentration was particularly critical of Ukrainian living conditions and folk beliefs. The last in a series of four articles, "Ruthenians in Western Canada: When Sickness Visits a Russian Home," centred on the problems confronting the Anglo-Saxon doctor as he sought to combat both sickness and superstitions. "Meeting the Needs on the Frontier: My Acquaintance with Lamont Hospital" discussed the role of that Methodist institution in eradicating traditional Ukrainian superstition and fatalistic acceptance of illness, thereby raising the standards of community health. The story of Nicholi, a Ruthenian youth (despite his impossible Ukrainian name) who would have died if primitive peasant remedies had been allowed to prevail, appeared in "Our Little Russian Brother," and concluded with Nicholi becoming a link between the old world and the new following his recovery. Elston's attitude in this regard closely paralleled that of the Protestant churches. The Anglo-Saxon could teach not only through the school but also by entering the home and ministering to physical needs; assimilation would occur naturally as example forced the recognition and rejection of antiquated practices and beliefs.[20]

Being a school teacher, Elston was naturally interested in educational work among Ukrainians, and once again the school, the Anglo-Saxon teacher, and the educational process were seen as primary Canadianizing bodies. Elston's writings on education in the Ukrainian districts of Alberta stressed the influence of the qualified Anglo-Saxon teacher both in the classroom and at home, the wisdom of English-language instruction, and the Ukrainians' active interest in the education of their children. Her articles included "Making Ruthenians into Canadians: An Interesting Experiment in Education," "English Schools for Foreigners in Alberta," and "The Russian in our Midst." The latter, more substantial than the rest, encompassed all aspects of life in the Ukrainian colony near Lamont — its distinguishing and picturesque features, traditions, material progress, the adoption of visible Canadian standards, and the characteristics of the people themselves. Some of Elston's most perceptive comments concerned what she considered typically Ukrainian traits — deep religiosity; suspicion of one another, particularly of those who prospered and rose above the norm; and distrust of new people and institutions.

The preceding discussion has involved the miscellaneous and less thematic literature on Ukrainians in Canada through World War I. Limited in length, range of subject matter, and depth of penetration, it formed the bulk of the material written on Ukrainians during these years. The resultant image of the Ukrainian, his background and present condition, was sketchy, being determined by Anglo-Canadians who were at best on the periphery of the coalescing Ukrainian-Canadian community and restricted to the visible and tangible. The accuracy of an individual's comments largely depended on his powers of observation and articulation, his knowledge, outlook, personal

11

prejudices, and ability to analyze. Specific research or concentration on Ukrainians as an identifiable and significant group in Canada was sporadic. Nevertheless, three publications in particular probed them in some detail and in relation to the question of assimilation confronting the two major Canadian institutions, the church and the school. Together they constitute the most enduring contribution to the body of literature on Ukrainians in Canada written in the period through World War I.

The sole work concerned exclusively with Ukrainians was a novel, *The Foreigner: A Tale of Saskatchewan,* by the Presbyterian clergyman Charles W. Gordon, who is better recognized by his literary pseudonym, Ralph Connor. Extremely prolific and popular as a novelist, Connor wrote numerous books on western Canada and on his home province of Ontario. Although he enjoyed a great reputation among his Canadian, British, and American contemporaries, and his western novels helped to stimulate British and central Canadian immigration to western Canada, he was not a good writer. Melodramatic plots and shallow characterizations served his central purpose of moralizing. Pitting Good against Evil with Good always triumphant, *The Foreigner* did not deviate from the wonted pattern. The novel operated on two levels: the lesser was that of the plot itself, while the greater developed a confrontation between the manly, virtuous, Christian Anglo-Saxon and the ignorant, emotional, and frequently immoral Galician. On this second level, Connor spoke independently on the value to Canada of the Galicians, and on the responsibility of Canadian churches and schools, to make them good Christians and good Canadians. In this respect *The Foreigner* was something of a fictional supplement to the annual reports on work among Galicians and Ruthenians to the general assembly of the Presbyterian Church of Canada.

The story commenced with a wedding celebration at the house of a Galician peasant woman, named Paulina Koval, in the predominantly Slavic colony of north end Winnipeg. The unexpected arrival of a mysterious stranger from Russia named Michael Kalmar, and his attempted murder of a Bukovinian named Rosenblatt, set the stage for the melodrama. A Russian nobleman and nihilist, Kalmar had escaped from imprisonment in Siberia to come to Canada where his motherless children were in the care of the dull-witted and slovenly Paulina. He was intent on settling old scores with his political enemies and traitors to the

Russian Fatherland, particularly Rosenblatt, who now financially controlled much of the Winnipeg Galician colony as well as Paulina's personal affairs. Although Kalmar's two children honoured the memory of their dead mother and respected their father and his ideals, as the novel progressed the children were transformed into "Canadians," and became the guiding lights for the Galician colony at Wakota in rural Saskatchewan where the action ends. To this colony gravitated all the major characters, including those Canadians responsible for introducing Christian and Anglo-Saxon virtues. Here too the senior Kalmar wreaked his final vengeance on Rosenblatt as the Russian intrigue built to its violent climax.

As this description of the inhabitants of north end Winnipeg illustrates, Connor understood little of the ethnic, political, or religious composition of eastern Europe:

> With a sprinkling of Germans, Italians, and Swiss, it was almost solidly Slav. Slavs of all varieties from all provinces and speaking all dialects were there to be found: Slavs from Little Russia and from Great Russia, the alert Polak, the heavy Croatian, the haughty Magyar, and occasionally the stalwart Dalmation from the Adriatic, in speech mostly Ruthenian, in religion orthodox Greek Catholic or Uniat [sic] and Roman Catholic.[21]

Errors abound. To begin with, Magyars are not Slavic but an Ugro-Finnian people whose closest relatives are located in the Ural Mountains. Secondly, of the nationalities named, only Little Russians or Ukrainians would speak Ruthenian, and only the Ukrainians of Galicia and Trans-Carpathia in the Austro-Hungarian Empire would be Uniate Christians. While conceding that their "non-discriminating Anglo-Saxon fellow citizens" called them all Galicians, Connor was no more knowledgeable himself. His own confusion made possible the marriage of Kalmar and Paulina, for it is highly improbable that a Russian nobleman would have married a Galician peasant woman, especially since they were separated geographically and politically into two empires. Similarly, it is illogical that Rosenblatt, being a Bukovinian, would have been employed in the Russian Secret Service and hence responsible for Kalmar's betrayal and arrest. Connor's ignorance of Russian nihilism and its historical applicability is equally evident. That Connor accorded the Russian Kalmar and his children a respect, dignity,   13 and intelligence not extended to Paulina and other Galicians, indicates that he made a distinction, however blurred, between the two. Yet somehow he has Kalmar inform his son that he is not of these Galician cattle, although he eventually becomes the leader of "his" people, the Galicians! The names of Kalmar's children — "Irma" and "Kalman" — were themselves typically Hungarian and most uncommon among both Ukrainians and Russians, once again revealing Connor's unfamiliarity with eastern Europe. Regardless of the confusing number of nationalities referred to, the fallacious statements, and the unlikely associations, it is obvious that Connor's story was basically concerned with Ukrainian immigrants.[22]

As contrived and absurd as its plot may have been, *The Foreigner* remains a significant document on the contemporary attitude of the Canadian evangelical Protestant clergy towards the assimilation of non-Anglo-Saxon immigrants. Here the contrast between the Christian Anglo-Saxon and the immoral Galician was most pronounced:

> Meanwhile, while respectable Winnipeg lay snugly asleep under snowcovered roofs and smoking chimneys, while belated revellers and travellers were making their way through white, silent streets and under avenues of snow-laden trees to homes where reigned love and peace and virtue, in the north end and in the foreign colony the festivities in connection with Anka's wedding were drawing to a close in sordid drunken dance and in sanguinary fighting. In the main room dance and song reeled on in uproarious hilarity. In the basement below, foul and fetid, men stood packed close, drinking while they could. It was for the foreigner an hour of rare opportunity. The beer kegs stood open and there were plenty of tin mugs about. In the dim light of a smoky lantern, the swaying crowd, here singing in maudlin chorus, there fighting savagely to pay off old scores or to avenge new insults, presented a nauseating spectacle.[23]

Critical of Galician moral standards, Connor attributed them not to an absolute moral character but to the centuries of moral development separating the Slavs from the Anglo-Saxons. He argued that an autocratic government and a retrograde and superstitious church in the homeland had spiritually and morally stunted them. Through his negative portrayal of Galicians

14　Connor undoubtedly sought to illustrate the danger to western

Canada if they were not assimilated and provided with the best Canadian ideals.

That the Slav was capable of improvement if given the opportunity is substantiated by the examples of Kalman and Irma, who rose above their origins through the positive influence of righteous Anglo-Saxons. Little Margaret Ketzel, who had learned the English language and Canadian ways at a Methodist mission and school, transformed Irma into an impressive young Canadian lady. Similarly, Kalman captured the attention of the ministering angel of the colony, a woman named Mrs. French, who devoted her life to the enlightenment and elevation of foreigners. While the efforts of the Methodist mission and Mrs. French were shown to be exemplary, Connor was pointed in his criticism of Anglo-Saxon Winnipeg for its neglect of foreign immigrants:

> Many and generous were the philanthropies of Winnipeg, but as yet there was none that had to do with the dirt, disease and degradation that were too often found in the environment of the foreign people. There were many churches in the city rich in good work, with many committees that met to confer and report, but there was not yet one whose special duty it was to confer and to report upon the unhappy and struggling and unsavory foreigner within their city gate.[24]

Mrs. French, battling this great indifference, did what she could. To remove Kalman from the streets of Winnipeg, she dispatched him to her brother-in-law in rural Saskatchewan. Jack French, although an excessive drinker, was Connor's ideal of manliness. Under his guidance and that of the Reverend Dr. Brown, who arrived to establish a Presbyterian mission, school, and hospital in an adjacent Galician colony, Kalman became a man, a Christian in the Presbyterian definition, and a good Canadian. His marriage to a Scottish girl indicated the route for fusing the many nationalities into one Canadian race.

Jack French and Dr. Brown represented two opposing reactions to the Galician immigrants.[25] French, after his initial overtures towards them had been repulsed, left them severely alone. If they were educated, he argued, they would soon run the country. Brown, on the other hand, contended that as they would soon run the country anyway, they had to be equipped for the task, for the existence of an undigested foreign mass could

15

jeopardize the future of western Canada. The two agencies to provide the Galicians with the necessary ideals were the church and the school. Brown claimed that it was the purpose of his church not to proselytize but to make good citizens. Nevertheless, the novel placed great emphasis on Kalman's conversion to Presbyterianism. Similarly the goodness and purity of Brown's religion was underlined by contrasting him with the corrupt and drunken Polish priest who appeared to grip the Galician colony.

The colony thrived partially because of the coal mine that Kalman discovered and developed to furnish employment for the Galicians, but the most crucial factor in its prosperity was the work of Brown and his mission:

> The changes apparent in the colony, largely as the result of Dr. Brown's labours, were truly remarkable. The creating of a market for their produce by the advent of the railway and for their labour by the development of the mine, brought the Galician people wealth, but the influence of Dr. Brown himself, and of his Home and of his Hospital, was apparent in the life and character of the people and especially of the younger generation. The old mud-plastered cabins were giving place to neat frame houses, each surrounded by its garden of vegetables and flowers. In dress the sheepskin and the shawl were being exchanged for the ready made suit and the hat of latest style. The Hospital, with its staff of trained nurses under the direction of the young matron, the charming Miss Irma, by its ministrations to the sick and more by the spirit that breathed through its whole service, wrought in the Galician mind a new temper and a new ideal. In the Training Home 50 Galician girls were being indoctrinated into that most noble of all sciences, the science of homemaking, and were gaining practical experience in all the cognate sciences and arts.[26]

Connor has here described the ideal program and goal of the Presbyterian Church in Christianizing and Canadianizing Galicians. When *The Foreigner* is divested of its intrigue and romance, it becomes apparent that its essential message and purpose was to examine the problem of the Slavic immigrant within Canada and to suggest a program for his assimilation from the evangelical Protestant point of view. That Connor's

degrading picture of Galicians negatively influenced public

opinion is verified by other writers.[27] Whether he convinced many
Anglo-Canadians to actively participate in the assimilation of
Galicians remains debatable.

The second major work to concern itself with Ukrainian
immigrants was also written from the evangelical Protestant
point of view, with emphasis on the role of Canadian Protestant
churches in Canadianizing the foreigner. James S. Woodsworth,
minister of the Methodist Church of Canada, wrote *Strangers
Within our Gates* in 1909. As superintendent of All People's
Mission in Winnipeg, he had personal contact with the many
peoples flocking to that city, and in *Strangers Within Our Gates*
proposed to acquaint Canadians with this "motley crowd" and to
impress upon the young, in particular, the numerous related
problems. The bibliography suggests that Woodsworth relied
greatly on American opinion, publications, and case studies for
his information on immigration and its attendant problems. He
attempted to equate these findings with the Canadian situation,
believing it to be a belated parallel of the American experience.
The danger to the Canadian nation posed by the influx of a
multitude of foreigners spurred J.W. Sparling, in his introduction
to the book, to strongly recommend it to his fellow Canadians:

> I can with confidence commend this pioneer Canadian work on
> this subject to the careful consideration of those who are
> desirous of understanding and grappling with this great and
> national danger. For *there is a danger and it is national!* Either
> we must educate and elevate the incoming multitudes or they
> will drag us and our children down to a lower level. We must see
> to it that the civilization and ideals of Southeastern Europe are
> not transplanted to or perpetuated on our virgin soil.[28]

Being concerned about the problem of developing a national
consciousness and identity among immigrants, the majority of
whom did not speak English, Woodsworth discussed the
following groups in terms of their desirability for Canada: British,
American, Scandinavian, German, French, Southeastern European, Austro-Hungarian, Balkan, Hebrew, Levantine, Italian,
Oriental, Negro, and Indian. We will restrict our discussion to
comments on those immigrants originating in southeastern
Europe or Austro-Hungary, as only they are relevant to this
survey of the literature on Ukrainians in Canada.

Woodsworth began his work by admitting that to most of his   17 contemporaries this area was a *terra incognita,* distinguished by a confusion of nationalities, languages, religions, and political allegiances. He looked at the Doukhobors and Lithuanians in some depth as composing a substantial proportion of the immigration from Russia, and examined the Bohemians, Slovaks, Poles, and Hungarians from Austro-Hungary. Those immigrants who called themselves "Russ" were Little Russians, "closely allied to the Rusniaks or Ruthenians of Galicia and Bukovina."[29] Recognizing a relationship between Little Russians and Ruthenians without realizing that they constituted one nationality, Woodsworth then examined them along with the Galicians under the heading of Austro-Hungary. The sections on Ruthenians, Poles, and Doukhobors were written by A.R. Ford of the Winnipeg *Telegram,* and therefore the views expressed in them cannot be directly attributed to Woodsworth. Nevertheless, the inclusion of Ford's articles without comment or criticism permits one to conclude that Woodsworth condoned his outlook and accepted his analysis.

Figuring disproportionately in court appearances, violent crimes, and in penitentiaries, the Ruthenian[30] had created a bad impression among the Canadians with whom he now resided. Ford commented: "Centuries of poverty and oppression have, to some extent, animalized him. Drunk, he is quarrelsome and dangerous. The flowers of courtesy and refinement are not abundant in the first generation of immigrants."[31] But the Galician provided much of the unskilled labor that was building Canada, and, while not overly enterprising as a farmer, he was making progress both agriculturally and educationally. "He is a patient and industrious workman. He is ambitious. He is eager to become Canadianized. He does not cling to a language which is rich in words that express sorrow and despondency and misery, and meagre in those that express aspiration and joy and hope. Above all, he yearns to get on the land and to own some acres of his own."[32]

The final chapters of *Strangers Within our Gates* dealt with immigration in general — its causes, effects, and restrictions; assimilation; and the challenge to the church. Disturbed by the racial, economic, social, and political effects of immigration on Canadian national life, Woodsworth favoured some form of restrictions that would exclude not only individuals but also certain classes. He referred specifically to Orientals, claiming that while mentally and physically fit they were displacing European labourers and were unassimilable. The assimilation of the desirable and adaptable races required the mobilization of various agencies: the church, the school, political clubs and organizations, the labour union, and both the English and native-language press. It was also imperative that Anglo-Canadians abandon their attitude of superiority and recognize the value in other languages and religions. "Loyalty to the old is the best guarantee of loyalty to the new"[33] was a theme to be adopted by later advocates of ethnic diversity, particularly in reference to such nationalistic groups as the Ukrainians.[34]

Turning to the challenge facing the churches, Woodsworth again focused on Ruthenians, both because their religious tradition was so divorced from his own experience and convictions, and because the Methodist and Presbyterian churches were active in Ukrainian missionary work. He characterized the religious tendencies of the Slav:

> The Slav is essentially religious, but his religious instincts have never yet found true expression. The move to the new land means a shaking of the very foundations of belief. The old associations are left behind, the mind is prepared for new impressions, the individual is thrown into an entirely different social life, and is enveloped by a different religious atmosphere. Sometimes he may cling tenaciously, desperately, to the old beliefs; often he renounces them entirely. Modifications must take place. The desire for light and liberty lies behind even the excesses into which some plunge. Light and liberty — these are what are needed.[35]

The Slavs ultimately had to work out their own salvation as reformation could proceed only from within, but meanwhile it was the churches' responsibility to preach, to educate, and to ameliorate existing social conditions.

As was the case with most English-language literature on Ukrainians in Canada, *Strangers Within our Gates* examined Ukrainians as one of many nationalities and in relation to the general Canadian issues of immigration and assimilation. *The Education of the New Canadian,* written in 1918 by James T.M. Anderson, Director of Education among New Canadians in Saskatchewan, was no exception. It also focused on the question of assimilation but from the educational standpoint. The adult immigrant, Anderson admitted, would never become a true

Canadian "imbued with the highest Anglo-Saxon ideals" as his habits, loyalties, and thought patterns would always remain those of the homeland. It was the New Canadian youth who were to be captured at their most impressionable age and equipped through the agencies of the public school and the Anglo-Saxon teacher for assuming their responsibilities as intelligent Canadian citizens.

The Education of the New Canadian was basically a manual for instruction in the English language and Canadian ideals for teachers employed in the foreign colonies of western Canada. In both urban ghettos and rural ethnic blocs, where Ruthenians, German Mennonites, and Doukhobors tended to predominate, the school was frequently the only Canadianizing force present, making the influence of Anglo-Saxon teachers of unquestionable character and patriotic dedication of paramount importance. Anderson wished to impress upon these teachers their duty to Canada and the British Empire and the magnitude of their task in assimilating non-English-speaking foreigners:

> Teachers! this is the kind of work required of you in the foreign settlements. You must get acquainted with these people of divers nationalities and interpret to them what our Canadian citizenship means. The solution of the racial problem lies almost wholly in your hands; the future of our glorious country largely depends upon your attitude on this national issue.[36]

Claiming impartiality and insight gained during ten years "intimate personal acquaintance" with different nationalities, Anderson commenced his study with a brief survey of the European background, life in Canada, and the progress of the numerically dominant groups — the Scandinavians, Slavs, and Germans. As the majority of the Slavs in Canada were Ruthenians from Galicia and Bukovina, he concentrated on them, examining their life in both Austria and Canada.[37] Writing at the close of World War I, Anderson was one of the first Anglo-Saxons to note that "Ukrainian" was the national designation of both Austrian Ruthenians and Little Russians. His conclusions regarding Ukrainians as potential Canadian citizens were optimistic in spite of his hostility towards the activities of certain priests and nationalist agitators to promote the Ukrainian language in the public schools. Anderson enumerated certain Slavic failings — a gross attitude towards sexual morality, a lack of collective wisdom, a tendency towards anarchy, a passivity in temperament, and a reluctance to accept the consequences of telling the truth — which did little to enhance the image of Ruthenians. Their redeeming qualities included a religious nature, a willingness to endure hardship, and a genius for self-expression.[38] There was no danger, however, that Slavic racial or religious ideals would preponderate in Canada, as they were those of a peasant culture and the second generation was rapidly transcending that milieu.

War had elevated Canada to nationhood, and national unity demanded the education and assimilation of non-English-speaking New Canadians. While a night school program could furnish the foreign adult population with the rudiments of English, citizenship ideals, and information on technical subjects, the public school was the primary vehicle for teaching English, disseminating knowledge on Canada, and inspiring patriotism for the new country. "This is the great melting pot into which must be placed the divers racial groups, and from which will eventually emerge the pure gold of Canadian citizenship."[39] Severely censuring the bilingual school system and half-educated foreign teachers — particularly the venture to train Ruthenian teachers in Manitoba and Saskatchewan — Anderson advanced the unilingual policy adopted among Ruthenians in Alberta as ideal. He advocated the "Direct Method" of teaching English (i.e., without the intermediary of the mother tongue) and provided concrete examples and lesson outlines. Many of his illustrations of the activities and methodology of individual teachers came from Ruthenian districts. In these illustrations the Anglo-Saxon teacher emerged as an enlightening missionary, and Anderson noted the positive response of Ruthenians when "a strong type of Canadian manhood or womanhood is placed in their midst."[40]

The Education of the New Canadian was written strictly from an Anglo-Saxon point of view that was determined to maintain the British character of Canada. Why the immigrant might wish to retain his language was never explored from an historical or a psychological perspective. The desire to have Ukrainian taught was attributed to the machinations of "priests and nationalist agitators"; Anderson doubted that it was rooted in the people themselves. The book's entire purpose was to examine how best to teach the non-Anglo-Saxon child to speak English and to venerate British-Canadian ideals and institutions. Education was not only for the child's sake but for the prosperity and security of

Canada. Anderson's emphasis on the indispensable function of the rural school and the principled Anglo-Saxon teacher in the process of assimilating non-British elements continued well into the inter-war period.

The first research specifically on Ukrainians was undertaken during World War I by the Bureau of Social Research for the governments of Manitoba, Saskatchewan, and Alberta, and directed by J.S. Woodsworth. The report of the investigation, "Ukrainian Rural Communities," appeared in January 1917. Unfortunately, it was never published and today only a few isolated copies exist.[41] Although it was an extensive work on contemporary conditions and developments in Ukrainian rural communities, the investigation did not survey all such communities in western Canada, but limited itself to certain districts thought to be typical: Stuartburn, Whitemouth and Brokenhead, Interlake, Sandy Lake, Dauphin, Canora, Insinger, Veregin, Vonda, Prince Albert, Hafford, Mundare, Shandro, Chipman, and Lamont.

The report consisted partly of comments by school teachers, educationalists, and Protestant missionaries serving in these communities, and included their observations of Ukrainian customs, traits, environment, and daily routine, and their assessment of material, educational, and spiritual progress. It was the assumption of the participants in the project that this approach would simultaneously eliminate the subjective factor and provide a more comprehensive view of a complex situation. It is noteworthy that an attempt was made to go beyond the perspective of the Anglo-Saxon observer; personal immigrant experiences were recorded in the report and, perhaps even more significantly, two Ukrainians officially assisted in its preparation. Ivan Petruschevich offered his suggestions and wrote a section on the history and potentiality of Ukrainians, while Wasyl Swystun was engaged as field investigator. In addition to a chapter on the historical background and traditions of Ukrainians, Swystun contributed the summaries on over half of the communities investigated. That Woodsworth, in his introduction to the report, drew on *Our Slavic Fellow Citizens* for an outline of Ukrainian history, indicated that he had increased his awareness of the legitimacy of the Ukrainian people as a national collectivity and had broken free of the stereotyped notions that characterized his *Strangers Within our Gates.*

From the data collected, "Ukrainian Rural Communities"

drew four conclusions:

> Our studies show (a) that the prosperity of the people is dependent to a large extent upon the character of the country in which they have settled; (b) that, on the whole, the immigrants remain isolated from their English-speaking neighbors; (c) that through the schools the children are being gradually "assimilated" but, in the process are losing much that should be retained; (d) that the educational, social, religious and, in general, the spiritual development is not proportionate to the material advancement.[42]

These conclusions suggested several outstanding needs of the Ukrainian rural communities: instruction in sanitation, home-making, and farming methods; medical assistance; religious education; citizenship training; special curricula for non-English-speaking immigrants; enforcement of school attendance; provision of the opportunity to learn English; protection against exploitation; and a unifying agency, such as the school, to initiate and organize social activities in every community. The report also advocated more careful screening of immigrants, a better system of distribution, closer settlement, assistance during the transitional period, and an improved rapport between Canadians and Ukrainian immigrants. Almost lost among the recommendations for aiding Ukrainians in adjusting to their Canadian environment was the proposal to encourage native handicrafts.[43]

"Ukrainian Rural Communities" was undoubtedly the pioneer English-language study in Ukrainian-Canadian historiography. It determined the location and the extent of Ukrainian rural communities in the three prairie provinces, and within that framework attempted a detailed characterization of conditions and developments in the Ukrainian settlements of western Canada. Unlike much of the other literature on Ukrainians in Canada written during this period, it systematically probed specific Ukrainian communities, recognizing their existence as identifiable entities in which Ukrainians lived and through which they would adapt to the Canadian environment. The underlying concept or motivation continued to be assimilation but without the pronounced emphasis on general Canadian objectives common in other contemporary works. Regrettably, this initial interest in the Ukrainian communities of western Canada was not sustained, and for almost two decades "Ukrainian Rural

Communities" was to be the sole study devoted exclusively to the development and history of Ukrainians in Canada.

Although considered subjects of Austria and treated as "enemy aliens" during World War I, Ukrainians were neither praised for their loyalty to Canada nor condemned for any treasonous actions in the infrequent references to them in the literature of those years.[44] The pastoral letter issued by Bishop Nicetas Budka of the Ukrainian Greek Catholic Church on July 27, 1914, urging his people to honour their military duty to the Austrian fatherland, was very strongly criticized even though Budka retracted his statements in a second letter on August 6.[45] Department of Education and Protestant missionary reports contained information on the attitudes and contributions to Canada's war effort in the various Ukrainian communities they served. Burgeoning Ukrainian nationalism was viewed with suspicion but there was generally little antagonism; as the war and the Russian Revolution progressed, Ukrainian hopes for an independent Ukraine were recognized.[46] For the most part, the events of World War I and the Ukrainian Revolution played an important role in educating Canadians about the Ukrainian historical experience.

In this first period of Ukrainian life in Canada, much of the literature on Ukrainians was purely descriptive, and explanatory attempts were made to identify and characterize a people unknown to Canadians. A growing understanding of the immigrants' European background could be discerned in Anglo-Saxon writings by the end of World War I, as they progressed from initial peasant stereotypes and vague definitions to more precise depictions of Ukrainian national development. Primarily concerned with the Ukrainians' impact on the political, economic, and social structure of Canada, representatives of Canadianizing institutions examined them in relation to major Canadian issues and the goal of national prosperity. With emphasis on assimilation from the point of view of Anglo-Saxon Canadians, little attention was paid to the development of a Ukrainian-Canadian society as a distinct and self-perpetuating entity. This reflected the embryonic state of this society and the fact that the Anglo-Saxon, except in rare instances, remained an observer on the outskirts of the vital happenings in the lives of Ukrainians. The Anglo-Saxon's interests did not promote the consolidation and perpetuation of a Ukrainian-Canadian

24 community which touched the larger Canadian scene only at

intervals. Consequently, his writings concentrated on measuring the progress of assimilation to Canadian ideals and standards, although occasionally comments anticipating the "mosaic" concept of Canadian identity also appeared.[47]

Assimilation Versus the "Mosaic"

Participation in the conflict of World War I launched Canada
into the inter-war era with new confidence in herself as a nation.
From the Anglo-Saxon point of view this reinforced the necessity
of assimilation, particularly with the resumption of mass
immigration. Although the vision of the Canadian nation
continued to be essentially British in character — largely to
counteract American pressures — greater maturity and faith in
herself permitted Anglo-Canada to evaluate seriously the
potential contribution of ethnically conscious non-British
nationalities to Canadian development. Gradually, the idea of a
"mosaic" acquired shape and depth, and Ukrainians were to play
a major role in the discussion that developed this new concept.[1]
The inter-war literature reflected this dual orientation. Not only
were individuals writing on Ukrainian-Canadian development,
but national Canadian bodies of various hues sponsored or
endorsed studies.

A second factor which had a positive effect on Ukrainian-
Canadian historiography was the increased familiarity of Anglo-
Saxon writers with Ukrainian Canadians. The longer Ukrainians
resided in Canada and the more established they became in
Canadian life, the greater was Anglo-Saxon contact with them. It
was therefore inevitable that Anglo-Canadians should broaden
their understanding of Ukrainians. Also significant were events
during World War I which briefly elevated the question of
Ukrainian national independence to international prominence.
Repercussions in Canada were apparent among Ukrainians, for
the Ukrainian and Russian Revolutions stimulated both the
crystallization of Ukrainian national consciousness and the
complex politicization of the Ukrainian-Canadian community.
Anglo-Saxon Canada reacted to both phenomena with trepida-
tion. The discussion of the Ukrainian question on the world stage

also enabled interested Anglo-Canadians to acquire knowledge of Ukrainian history hitherto unobtainable. Their first post-war writings demonstrated the favourable impact of this knowledge on their assessment and definition of the Ukrainians in Canada.

The evolution in general Canadian understanding of Ukrainian identity and its historical development is most strikingly evident in an author whose writings bridged the war years. In 1919 Miriam Elston continued to publish her articles on Alberta Ukrainians, stressing their educational, material, and spiritual progress, and their adaptation to Canadian ways. She utilized Ukrainian enlistment figures and contributions to the Patriotic and Red Cross Funds to prove their assimilation, patriotism, and desire to be integrated into the Canadian community. Although Elston still used "Russian" and "Ruthenian" interchangeably, she revealed a vague awareness of her error:

> In Canada the Russian and his brother, the Russo-Austrian, were usually, in pre-war days, spoken of collectively as Ruthenians. Most of the Russians in Canada are what are known as Low Russians, a name given to the peasant of Southern Russia. The majority of the Austrians in Canada are, in reality, Russo-Austrians, that is, they are blood brothers to the Low Russians — a part of the Low Russian people who have overflowed the boundaries of Austria. Their language, with slight provincial differences, is the one language. Their manners, their habits, their customs, are very similar.[2]

In a second article written in 1919, Elston first used the word "Ukrainian" and intimated that conditions for which she had previously condemned Ukrainians were not really their fault but were rooted in history:

> When we recount the history of the Ukrainian race in Canada, we realize that we are recounting the history of a people who have, under rather adverse circumstances, made good. The first and foremost of these adverse circumstances have been dire poverty, ignorance and the superstition that always stalks beside ignorance. As a people they have not been responsible for any of these conditions. They are but the natural outcome of the oppression under which they have lived in the old land.[3]

Thus, the physical and psychological obstacles that Ukrainians had to date successfully surmounted, made them doubly admirable as a people.

27

Frances Swyripa

An article by F. Heap, also in 1919, in many respects paralleled the tone of Elston's post-war publications. Heap also underlined expressions of Ukrainian loyalty to Canada and the British Empire during the Great War, and noted their agricultural and educational progress. He also provided an abbreviated but faulty sketch of Ukrainian national history, totally omitting the Polish influence on Ukrainian development. Heap was the first Anglo-Saxon to mention organizations within the Ukrainian community, reporting the establishment of Ukrainian boarding schools, libraries, reading societies, and musical and dramatic associations. Of Ukrainian nationalism in Canada, he harboured little fear:

> Their nationalism in so far as they can be said to display any, is unlike French or Quebec nationalism, in that it has no ulterior designs of separate government or political supremacy, and is confined practically to protection, co-operation and mutual helpfulness, and ambition to "do well" as a class, and cannot be said to amount to even excessive clannishness.[4]

As Ukrainians entered the post-war era, their high naturalization rate and participation in municipal and school government indicated their desire to become a permanent and active segment of the Canadian community. It was an opportune time for a more cordial attitude towards them on the part of government and public bodies, Canadian clubs and church groups, employers and individuals.

The reports on Ukrainian mission work presented to the General Assembly of the Presbyterian Church in Canada after 1918 and prior to church union in 1925, also revealed a greater knowledge of the Ukrainian past and contemporary situation in Europe than had existed before the outbreak of war.[5] At the same time, alarm was expressed at the growing manifestations of Ukrainian nationalism in Canada. The previously stringent tone regarding the total assimilation of Ukrainians to Anglo-Saxon ideals, institutions and ways of life, however, was considerably modified. Traditional Ukrainian antagonism to assimilation was better understood, resulting in a more receptive attitude towards the concept of a composite nationality for Canada:

> The word "assimilate" which they [the Ukrainians] have grown to hate means for them extinction. What the best of them are

contending for, is not that they should be absorbed and simply lose their identity, but that they should be allowed to come in as partners in this great community of races in Canada and to make their contribution in blood and in character and endowment to the new nation that shall arise in our great land. As a matter of fact their contention is our own view point. Whether we like to admit it or not these people are partners with us making contributions in blood and character in the new life of this nation. The wisest thing to do, would seem to me is to admit them as such, to accept what is best and overcome as far as possible what is unworthy of good citizens by teaching them the best that we ourselves know and prize highly. All our efforts to keep separate from them will be just as futile as their efforts to keep separate from us. And we are learning every day what a great contribution they are able to made. Like ourselves they are real democrats and have often paid the supreme price to advocate their principles. Like ourselves they believe in the necessity of an educated citizenship and many years ago they had in their native land among the best systems of education to be found in Europe. Through the medium of our School Home we are having practical demonstration of the fact that in ability to acquire, in serious application to work, the children of the New Canadian will equal if not surpass our own children.[6]

While this statement was a personal opinion and not an official Presbyterian pronouncement, it was echoed in 1924 in another report to the General Assembly on Ukrainian work:

The people are warned of the danger of being absorbed in the cosmopolitan life of Canada and the disappearanc of every national characteristic peculiarly Ukrainian. It seems difficult to persuade the Ukrainian people that they are making a distinct contribution to the character and quality of Canadian life. All racial groups must come to see that nationality in Canada is not the gift of any one people but the sum of the qualities of more than 60 different nations in their representatives who share in common the inheritance of this land.[7]

Even so, as immigration from continental Europe resumed, assimilation remained the dominant theme in Anglo-Saxon writings about Ukrainians in Canada. In 1920 William G. Smith published *A Study in Canadian Immigration,* endorsed by the

29

Canadian National Committee for Mental Hygiene.[8] From an analysis of past practices, Smith's study provided guidelines for a prudent immigration policy to be adopted by Canada in the 1920s to ensure national prosperity and health. Although it focused on the history of Canadian immigration in general and included recommendations for improved immigration laws, it also considered individual racial groups as an integral component of the immigration question.

Like other post-war writers, Smith emphasized the agricultural progress made by Ukrainians with negligible government assistance, their advancement in education, their demonstrations of loyalty through enlistments during the war, and the fact that they were learning English and adopting Canadian ways. As new ideas slowly penetrated the Ukrainian colonies, assimilation proceeded apace. Although Smith gleaned much of his factual information from American statistics and situations, he also provided Canadian figures and percentages by nationality for mental and physical defectives, illiteracy, and crime. His data could only be applied to Ukrainians in a limited way as they were grouped together with Austro-Hungarians or Russians.

Smith alluded to a "composite nationality" but continued to stress assimilation through assistance, goodwill, friendship, and acceptance of the best of what the immigrant had to offer to established Canadians. The cultivation of a new national spirit was essential but did not demand the complete renunciation of previous loyalties:

> But the cultivation of that national spirit which is Canada need not in the slightest interfere with the tender memories that remain in the heart of the new citizen for the land of his birth. Desire to live and serve under a new flag does not require that a man hate the one under which he was born. Nowhere does that apply more forcibly in Canada at the present time than among those Slavic peoples whose compatriots, like the Poles, Ukrainians and others are trying to fashion new nations amid the welter of Europe.[9]

Notwithstanding the above, Smith's concept of Canada was clearly British in character. He closed with a plea to young patriotic Canadians to "man the outposts of Canadian nationality" in the schools, educating the immigrant for the future, and thereby completing the building of a national superstructure whose foundations had been humbly laid by their forefathers.

In 1922 Smith wrote a related study, *Building the Nation: The Churches' Relation to the Immigrant,* as the last in a series of mission-study textbooks that were sponsored by the Methodist, Presbyterian, and Congregationalist churches of Canada. From the basic contention that the church was an indispensable factor in building the Canadian nation and forging a national spirit, Smith outlined its role in the process of Canadianizing the non-English-speaking immigrants and developing among them a common devotion to Canada. It could best fulfil its duty through three primary channels — the school and teacher, the hospital and doctor, the Bible and evangelist. By recruiting and training young Canadians for service in these fields, it would discharge its obligations. Although the British connection and Anglicization of the foreigner were now superseded by the urgent need to create a Canadian national spirit, the three avenues of pursuit by the Canadian Protestant churches echoed the policies that they had adopted to Anglicize and Christianize Ukrainian immigrants in the first two decades of the twentieth century.

In *Building the Nation* Smith dealt much more extensively with Ukrainians than he had in *A Study in Canadian Immigration.* Concerned as it was with the development of Canadian unity, *Building the Nation* considered Ukrainian nationalism in some detail, for the fate of Ukraine inevitably evoked a response in Canada. Polish-Ukrainian animosity, originating in Europe but transferred to and perpetuated in Canada, was a case in point. Smith felt that the cultivation of a Canadian national spirit was all the more necessary since a common loyalty to Canada would bury such ancient hatreds. Suggesting that the twentieth century could conceivably witness the realization of Ukrainian hopes for independence, he described the character of Ukrainian nationalism:

Lack of political unity seems to have intensified the desire for nationality, and through the vicissitudes of years, inspired by tradition, poets and historians, there has grown the hope that the land of the Ukraine would one day be the land of a free and independent people taking their place among the nations of Europe. It is this slumbering fire of nationalism which today is growing into the demand for political and geographical unity, and seeking recognition in the councils of the world. This is the   31 spirit which may be found more or less in evidence in various communities of Ukrainians in Canada, in the spirit of "nationalism."[10]

Smith was not, however, alarmed by or critical of its manifestation among Ukrainian Canadians:

> The eager desire of the Ukrainian living in Canada for the freedom and nationality of his own people in Europe — so called nationalism — may, unfortunately, be regarded as un-Canadian or anti-Canadian; and it need not be denied that this is possible or actual. But eagerness for the national independence of the land and people of one's fathers is not inseparably connected with hostility to the land of one's residence or adoption. Rather devotion to one is the promise and potency of devotion to the other.[11]

Canadianization encompassed both the adoption of the external traits of Canadian life and the development of a devotion to the new country. While the Ukrainians in Canada had prospered economically and embraced Canadian ways in their outward and visible forms, their emotional and patriotic assimilation remained in abeyance.

In contrast to Smith's two studies which superficially discussed Ukrainians in Canada as elements of general Canadian issues, other works appeared during the 1920s which more intensively scrutinized their assimilation and progress. Frank Yeigh, for example, wrote an article in 1922 which illustrated the process of assimilation by singling out individual immigrants of various nationalities who had successfully penetrated and adapted to the Canadian world. Educational progress and subsequent public service were cited as characteristics of good citizenship. Yeigh's confidence in the role of the Anglo-Saxon teacher and the Presbyterian Christian influence in Canadianizing Ukrainian youths was most pronounced. Although it was the author's expressed purpose to eradicate erroneous convictions held by certain Anglo-Saxons that the foreigner was ignorant and illiterate — Yeigh spoke from the belief that a new attitude towards non-Anglo-Saxons in Canada was timely — the article conveyed the impression that he too considered the foreigner elevated in the process of becoming Canadian.[12]

32   One of the first theses to examine Ukrainians in Canada was

submitted to the University of Alberta in 1925. "The Rural School as a Community Centre: A Discussion Dealing with the Problem of the Assimilation of New Canadians in Western Canada" by John W. McAllister, was McAllister's personal record of how he as a teacher transformed the Angle Lake School in northeastern Alberta into the centre of educational, social, and recreational activities for the entire community. Although a decidedly unscholarly thesis, it is now interesting as an example of the actual implementation of the Anglo-Canadian program to make the rural public school the vital focal point of a foreign district. With Ukrainians constituting one-half of the population in the area under study and the school itself straddling the border between the extensive Ukrainian colony to the west and the English settlement to the east, McAllister noted that "the problem of handling the school successfully . . . included . . . very careful treatment of international, political and religious questions in order to bind this cosmopolitan settlement into one co-operative unit."[13] He failed, however, to reveal how he had tackled the problem. McAllister concentrated on concrete details — the development of a playground, school garden, experimental station, sports, competitions, attractive landscaping, and the social gatherings around the school. With little direct or theoretical reference to the question of assimilating New Canadians, McAllister attempted to show how an active community school under a wise and dedicated teacher could facilitate and promote the process.

In a series of articles published in 1928 under the title *The Value to Canada of the Continental Immigrant,* Peter H. Bryce, for twenty years the chief medical officer of the Federal Immigration Service, examined Ukrainian economic progress and, to a lesser degree, social and educational advances. Bryce had toured western Canada in 1927 to investigate changes wrought among the continental immigrants in the two decades he had been responsible for admitting them. By illustrating through specific examples, tables, and statistics, the material and social progress and the assimilation of settlers, his book supported continued continental immigration. It was perhaps also a rebuttal to those who would have restricted such immigration on the grounds that it retarded Canadian national development. Bryce mentioned in particular those "in high places, as in the Church, who allow themselves at times to be carried away by their prejudices, uttering words unworthy of their station and calling."[14]

33

The initial chapters of Bryce's brochure were a travelogue describing conditions as he witnessed them in several colonies established by different nationalities. In a characteristically anecdotal manner he provided concrete examples of Ukrainian material accomplishments drawn from across western Canada, noting in contrast the Interlake district of Manitoba which would have been better left in its virgin state. Conceding that his survey was limited in scope, Bryce nevertheless considered his general conclusions to be valid:

> In a word, we see everywhere in the three provinces of Manitoba, Saskatchewan and Alberta that the continental immigrants have remained agriculturists to the extent of at least 75% of their total numbers, performed the tasks essential to the prosperity of the towns and cities there and of Canada, and are giving themselves gladly to the building up of great prosperous communities and provinces where, quite properly, native-born British Canadians in large measure guide the ship of state toward her destined haven of nationhood.[15]

The distinction between the respective roles of the British Canadian and the continental immigrant in attaining Canada's national destiny is clear. Convinced as he was of the superiority of the Anglo-Saxon, in presenting what was essentially an economic argument in favour of continental immigration, Bryce readily acknowledged that Ukrainains and other immigrants had been invaluable to Canada in the development of her resources.

In the early 1920s the Masonic Order of Saskatchewan established a War Memorial Scholarship Fund for teachers who contracted to teach at least a year in one of the "more backward non-English-speaking districts" of that province. Two-thirds of the districts chosen were predominantly Ukrainian. One of the selected teachers who, by his own admission, spent "three happy years" in one such district, was Robert England, later to become continental superintendent of the colonization department of the CNR. In 1929, on the basis of his own experiences and the detailed reports submitted by scholarship teachers regarding their observations of daily life, conditions in the community, overall progress, traditions, and racial characteristics of the people among whom they had been located, England published a study on the assimilation of continental immigrants entitled *The Central European Immigrant in Canada.* In its emphasis on the role of the public school in assimilating the non-Anglo-Saxon, the book was a successor to Anderson's *The Education of the New Canadian.*

As the teachers were said to be "intimately acquainted" with conditions in their respective communities — their comments being based on primary evidence and not on hearsay or prejudiced opinion — the Masonic Order asserted that England's book "should prove the most authoritative document on Canadianization problems ever issued in Canada."[16] England himself claimed to treat the subject objectively and without bias. One must remember, however, that the teachers on whose statements he relied were themselves amateur observers. Little trained in immigrant psychology and ignorant of the European background of the people in their districts, they were bound mentally by the attitudes and prejudices of their time and were often alien figures in frequently close-knit communities. Their comments cannot be accepted unconditionally.

The first section of the book outlined the problem of assimilating central Europeans. Concerned about the possibility of the British in Canada being overwhelmed and their standard of living, political, economic and social creeds endangered, England commented upon the situation in Saskatchewan: "Allowing for the preponderance of British stock in towns and villages, it is quite reasonable to conclude *that British stock is outnumbered in northern rural Saskatchewan by two to one.*"[17] This fact underscored the magnitude of the task confronting the scholarship teachers entering unfamiliar and difficult to penetrate communities where remnants of medieval civilization persisted.

England's own descriptions of Ukrainians abounded in stereotypes and generalizations. In their native land, England contended, they were unenterprising, unambitious, and impractical, preferring alcohol and gambling to work. Goitre was common, cleanliness not esteemed, and parasites tolerated. Some of his statements bordered on the absurd:

Passing through the crowded market, one notices a feature now a commonplace in Western Canada, that the Ruthenians seem to stand closer together, and make hotter, denser groups than most other people. This, however, is more marked in the case of the Jews.

Such a remark obliges one to accept England's other observations 35 with reservations. Describing Ukrainians as the most backward of the Slavs but independent and nationalistic, he added that they venerated their language, traditions, and history, and had maintained their dream of an autonomous state.[18]

The second part of England's study dealt with the Masonic project itself. It provided numerous accounts of social and economic conditions in non-English districts served by the scholarship teachers and delineated the vital influence of the rural school, including its future potential as a community centre under the guidance of a patriotic and dedicated Anglo-Saxon teacher. Ostensibly, the authors of the project thought of the community as a unit in which the economic organization, school, church, home, club, and cultural background of its members were viewed in interaction; in actuality it considered the non-indigenous school, largely to the exclusion of other forces, as the primary and pivotal factor. England referred briefly and favourably to German, Scandinavian, French-speaking, and Mennonite districts, then turned to those predominantly Ukrainian as they constituted the majority of the localities involved in the project.

The picture created of conditions in Ukrainian communities was in general negative. England was not overly optimistic about Ukrainian social and economic progress, and his criticism of agricultural development contrasted sharply with the very positive statements of other contemporary writers:

> Pioneer conditions are to be expected in the newer districts, but it will come as a shock to most to realise the small amount of economic progress that has been made in some older districts, where the population is Slav in origin. In all districts the gardens are well kept and productive, so that it would appear that the Southeastern peasant's initial difficulty lies in accommodating himself to the larger farming unit of Western Canada.[19]

Although England conceded that the successful had prevailed against great obstacles, many of his statements, in addition to those of the scholarship teachers, were both uncharitable and questionable as they reflected the opinions and presumptions of an outsider only superficially acquainted with the inner life of Ukrainians.[20] Children, he declared, were overworked, and

women were underprivileged slaves of their husbands.[21] He

claimed Ukrainians did not appreciate social organization and revealed negligible evidence of sportmanship or an *esprit de corps*. Owing to their unsavory hygienic traditions, health conditions among them were inevitably poor. England concluded: "All the scholarship teachers' reports give evidence of unsatisfactory conditions in the house and on the farm."[22] As much of the economic and social backwardness witnessed in Ukrainian communities was due to a lack of education, the rural school staffed by an Anglo-Saxon teacher was an essential vehicle of enlightenment.

The school was not to be "a monastic institution divorced from the pursuits and interests of the community." A capable teacher could "make the rural school what the church has been, an institution loved by all, respected by all — a great moral as well as educational power in the land,"[23] and the focal point for the domestic, social, physical, intellectual, and economic life of a community. Although England recognized that the school in a non-English district was an alien institution not readily accepted by or identified with the community, he continued to stress the role of the Anglo-Saxon teacher as a community leader, who was "determining attitudes, inculcating habits, suggesting ideals, fostering hope, giving perspectives." He was to be an exemplary influence on the foreign mind, conveying "Anglo-Saxon ideas of sportsmanship and service," concepts of chivalry, courage, courtesy, and kindness, and "the humaneness of the Anglo-Saxon," as though the Anglo-Saxon people enjoyed a monopoly of such qualities. England's vision of the role of the Anglo-Saxon teacher in a foreign settlement was perhaps unrealistic and idealistic, for he generally remained on the periphery of integral religious, social, and cultural activities.

The final section of England's book was more theoretical, examining the psychology of assimilation and outlining the practical problems of immigration, assimilation, and educational administration with special reference to the situation in western Canada. Opposing coercion in Canadianization or assimilation, England stated:

We cannot compel people to accept our standards, our customs or our ways. The work of assimilation must not be a work of putting into bondage. It must be a task of emancipation. It must be a challenge and a call to wider perspectives, saner ideals, better habits and customs, but greater responsibility.[24]

37

England's fascination with the idea of progress caused him to encourage the rejection of much of what he saw in the central European peasant's heritage and psychology — "patriarchal and ecclesiastical authority, parochialism, attachment to the soil, and inferiority complex through political disabilities, underprivileged women and children, primitive methods sanctioned by tradition."[25] Equally objectionable were an immaturity and a limited capacity for continued mental growth. Progress was feasible only through the goodwill and co-operation of both old and new Canadians, seeking their roots in loyalty to the community and gradually expanding to promote unity and progress on a national scale. England observed:

> Canada has a great opportunity, as a residuary legatee of British ideals of tolerance and fair play on the North American continent, to be the interpreter and reconciler of a new world. Our great land, with its diverse races and double culture challenges our political sagacity and courage to be on the side of the forward looking forces. If we fumble with our message in the world, what Science calls Progress and the theologian God, will find another messenger.[26]

In general, England provided a derogatory image and assessment of Ukrainians and their communities in western Canada. The excerpts from the reports of the scholarship teachers bear the stamp of spectators who examined Ukrainians outside of their cultural context and judged them according to an alien set of standards. While some historical background was given on other groups anxious to preserve much of their heritage in Canada — notably the Doukhobors and Mennonites — there was very little work of a similar nature done on Ukrainians, their European background being described solely in terms of their picturesque villages and unique customs. Of course, the scholarship teachers had the right to their own comments and opinions, but the information they provided could hardly be considered very authoritative or objective. England's book is useful as a record of Ukrainian character, habits, customs, and conditions of daily life as viewed through Anglo-Saxon eyes. Its chief contribution, however, to English-language literature on Ukrainians in Canada is its function in articulating the role of the rural public school and Anglo-Saxon teacher in Canadianizing and assimilating the non-English-speaking immigrant and his children.

With the publication of *The Central European Immigrant in Canada,* official and semi-official interest in the contemporary problem of Canadianizing and assimilating non-Anglo-Saxons through the agencies of the rural public school and the Anglo-Saxon teacher reached its zenith. Henceforth, literary activity in this field was removed to the arena of university research. Emphasis was increasingly placed on specific, limited, and practical problems or projects that were not particularly concerned with utilizing either the school or teachers as vehicles of assimilation.

In the inter-war period official Methodist and Presbyterian interest and involvement with Ukrainians also waned. In 1929 the Reverend Alexander J. Hunter wrote the major work to emerge from Protestant missionary labours among the Ukrainians. Endorsed by the United Church of Canada as a study text and an account of its missionary work in western Canada, *A Friendly Adventure* was, narrowly speaking, the record of Hunter's own efforts and achievements during twenty-five years as a Presbyterian minister, doctor, advisor, and friend of Ukrainians at Teulon, Manitoba. On a wider plane it was an illustration of the successful penetration of a Ukrainian community by a Canadian Protestant church largely through the overtures of a sympathetic representative.[27] Contrary to the tenor of much of the related literature published by the Presbyterian Church, which interwove Canadianization in the Anglo-Saxon mould with evangelical Christianization, Hunter's theoretical appeal to Ukrainians was Christian before it was Canadian. He pointed out the error "of identifying our own national traits [British-Canadian] with essence of Christian faith."[28] As an idealistic Christian Hunter sought to understand Ukrainians historically, intellectually, and emotionally.

He devoted considerable space to the religious traditions and history of Ukrainians, emphasizing, as did others of his training and inclination, the wrongful use of religion as a political tool, the error in ritualistic forms of worship, and the view that the Greek Catholic Church was an authoritative dictatorial body. Even so, he was far more sympathetic to Ukrainians than were most of his contemporaries. Concerning the ritual of the Ukrainian church service, Hunter commented:

> Seeing that ritual carried out in a little country church, one could realize what its grandeur might be in some great

39

cathedral of the old world, with trained singers and thousands of worshippers. The Roman ritual pales before it and the Anglican becomes almost invisible. Such a ritual befits a mighty empire whose subjects are to be inspired, not to reason why, but only to do — and die.

I do not love ritualism, yet if I were ever to become a ritualist I think I should prefer the Greek Church.[29]

Similarly, he grasped the association between nationality and religious loyalty manifest among Ukrainians and the significance to them of the Greek Catholic Church as a national institution. He explained this phenomenon to his Anglo-Canadian readers through an analogy illustrating the Anglican's national allegiance to the Church of England.[30] In both instances, loyalty to the church symbolized loyalty to the nation.

Hunter denied that it was the intention of his church to proselytize on behalf of Presbyterianism. Its goal was solely to help Ukrainians become more intelligently Orthodox or Catholic. Nevertheless, he discussed in some detail the development and goals of the Independent Greek Church and the motives behind Presbyterian sponsorship. Some indication of the antagonism encountered by the Presbyterian Church and its Independent Greek protégé can be gleaned from Hunter's references to the work of Bolshevik propaganda, and, more importantly, because they exerted a much greater impact on Ukrainians, of nationalist agitators who strove to denounce and vilify both the Presbyterian and Independent Greek churches as English assimilative organs. Hunter's resentment of Ukrainian nationalist leaders who hindered his work at Teulon was thinly veiled. In turn, however, he was able to justify Ukrainian resistance to assimilation on historical grounds:

For centuries the Ukrainians have been struggling against assimilation by the Poles on the one side and the Russians on the other, so they were very easily aroused by such a cry.... That word "assimilate" has a terrible significance to the Ukrainian patriot. He understands that the lion assimilates the lamb when he eats him and is resolved that his people shall not be assimilated in that way.[31]

Conversely, Hunter felt that the seemingly ingrained loyalty of Ukrainians to race and land would ultimately be transferred to
40 Canada.

Hunter's refusal to equate Canadianization with the adoption of evangelical Christianity permitted him to approach Ukrainians in terms of brotherhood and helpfulness, not doctrine, and from the standpoint of social Christianity — practice not theory — regardless of creed. This attitude also enabled him to evaluate the success of Presbyterian mission work among Ukrainians without counting converts:

> Here we need to clear our mind of possible confusion. Our aim is not primarily to strengthen our own particular denomination at the expense of other denominations. We wish, most of all, to bring about brotherly relations in a Christian spirit between the different races. We hold certain views about the Christian life and about the significance of the Christian religion that we wish our new friends to understand. If they are satisfied with our views and would like to work with us in our organization, we shall be very glad to have them with us, but we want them still to feel that we are comrades even though working under some other religious organization. To most of us, I think, religious organizations are merely implements for serving the religious life. The real Church is the invisible communion of kindred spirits.[32]

Hunter's approach to Ukrainians was universally Christian before it was either Presbyterian or Canadian. In addition, his knowledge and appreciation of the Ukrainian people — their history and their literary tradition — as well as his intimate acquaintance with the structure and dynamics of a Ukrainian community in Canada, far exceeded that revealed in the writings of his Anglo-Saxon contemporaries who entered Ukrainian communities as representatives of other Anglo-Canadian institutions.

Hunter's intellectual interest in Ukrainian history and literature was exceptional, but the second trend to emerge in the English-language literature of the 1920s on Ukrainians in Canada reflected this development on a more popular level. The crystallizing concept of a "mosaic" definition of Canadian national identity forced its proponents to examine both the psychological traits and cultural backgrounds of the various immigrant groups in Canada. This not only laid bare the diverse national historical experiences which shaped the attitudes and outlooks of New Canadians, but also provided direction as to   41 what facets of a group's heritage should be preserved and perpetuated for the enrichment of Canada. It was no longer sufficient that the non-Anglo-Saxon be encouraged to appreciate British-Canadian ideals, laws, and institutions and to acquire a knowledge of the English language while excluding his own heritage from his daily life. Some Canadians began to realize that the immigrants possessed spiritual and cultural treasures from civilizations far older than Canada's and were capable of sharing them with all Canadians. In 1922 one commentator observed the following regarding the legacy of the foreign immigrant:

> In the first place he has a stick-to-it-iveness, a persistency and an anxiety to do things well. Handicraft work we know nothing of and yet these people bring a complete knowledge of many handicrafts. Culture too they bring in the form of literature, folk music, and folk dances, all of which we are lacking in. A neighborliness and a desire to bear one another's burdens is characteristic of many of them. Thus we see that they have no small contribution to make to our national life.[33]

When applying the "mosaic" concept to specific nationalities in Canada, Anglo-Canadians were restricted by their unfamiliarity with immigrant backgrounds and traits. Hence, they were often unaware of the fact that the foreign cultures they were exposed to were usually those of the peasant classes, which formed the bulk of the immigration. This was certainly the case with the Ukrainians, for it was the Ukrainian peasant culture—characterized by its attachment to the soil, its traditions and rituals determined by the natural cycles of life, and its colourful handicrafts and folk songs — that the Anglo-Saxon encountered and considered as the Ukrainian contribution to Canada's cultural "mosaic." The Ukrainian literary heritage was precluded by the language barrier and the national historical experience rendered insignificant by the lack of Ukrainian sovereignty.[34] Therefore, the contemporary literature analyzing the Ukrainian component of the Canadian "mosaic" predictably reflected the peasant orientation of the Ukrainians in Canada.

The term "mosaic" was introduced and defined in 1926 by Kate A. Foster in a publication entitled *Our Canadian Mosaic*. Foster described the purpose of her study in the following manner: "to make available in easily accessible form accurate information in regard to those who come from other lands to establish new homes for themselves in Canada, and to stimulate interest in a problem of prime importance to our national life."[35] Even though it popularized the "mosaic" concept, *Our Canadian Mosaic* was still primarily concerned with the assimilation of non-Anglo-Saxons, devoting considerable space to a discussion of the activities and services of various Canadian institutions working to facilitate Canadianization. Foster's definition of assimilation, however, did not reiterate the previous emphasis on Anglo-conformity:

> One hears much in these days about the impossibility of assimilating certain peoples into our national life — but have we TRIED? — And are we prepared to try? In many minds the term "assimilation" is confused with amalgamation. Does the former necessarily imply intermarriage — the fusion of races? Is not assimilation rather the incorporation into our national life of all people within our borders for their common well-being. Is it not the working together side by side for the common advancement, each race contributing something of value and so slowly but surely evolving a new people enriched by the diversity of its origin?[36]

This view of assimilation is at the core of Foster's definition of the Canadian mosaic.

That Ukrainians, Foster contended, had preserved through centuries of national oppression a love of their culture and a devotion to their homeland, signified the potential for a similar loyalty to Canada. Her discussion of the Ukrainian element in Canada included a brief analysis of three factors active in the integration of Ukrainians into Canadian life. The public school, the Canadian church, and the social organizations had been traditionally advocated by Anglo-Saxon exponents of assimilation. For the first time, however, Ukrainian organizations were referred to not as unhealthy perpetuators of old loyalties but as useful mechanisms for easing integration. During the 1930s Anglo-Saxon researchers into Ukrainian-Canadian life were to expand on this novel idea.

With the concept of a "mosaic" came increased interest in the various non-British cultures of Canada. Reflecting this development, in 1928 John M. Gibbon, in his capacity as general publicity agent for the Canadian Pacific Railway, organized a series of folk festivals across Canada, featuring immigrant songs, 43 dances, and handicrafts. These festivals, in the opinion of one observer, were the first attempt "to demonstrate to Canadians that these newcomers from Europe possessed characteristic spiritual qualities which might be made to enrich the national life"[37] and which had gone unnoticed up to this time. Foreign immigrants were not simply ignorant manual labourers but the heirs of a variety of cultural skills that formed an integral part of their existence. Gibbon himself argued that the preservation and dissemination of the folk cultures of the different nationalities in Canada would greatly enliven a rather monotonous Canadian scene. His folkloristic studies culminated in the publication of *Canadian Mosaic: The Making of a Northern Nation,* an elaboration of a series of CBC radio broadcasts in 1938 that featured the folk music of various national groups in Canada.

Gibbon claimed that to understand the Canadian people one required a knowledge of their history and the European countries from whence they came. This was all the more imperative as a standardized Canadian type had yet to emerge from the racial conglomerate brought together in one country:

> The Canadian people today presents itself as a decorated surface, bright with inlays of separate colored pieces, not painted in colors blended with brush or palette. The original background in which the inlays are set is still visible but these inlays cover more space than that background, and so the ensemble may truly be called a mosaic.[38]

Gibbon was acutely aware of the value of the ethnic and cultural "mosaic" in Canada, its individual segments cemented together by community interests, social organizations, and the school. For each racial group discussed in *Canadian Mosaic,* he provided a sketch of their historical development, settlement in Canada, personal contributions by members of the group to Canadian life, and the general contribution of each group as determined by a stereotyped image. Gibbon quoted extensively from diaries, newspapers, books, speeches, and reports written by immigrants themselves, their descendants, or one of the numerous authorities on a particular group or aspect of assimilation. He also included statements by some members of the present generation of each nationality to indicate its attitude towards Canada and the vision it had of its role in national development. Gibbon described

Ukrainians as a nation of poets, musicians, and artists whose representatives had proven to be a physical asset to Canada and were now anxious to acquaint Anglo-Saxons with their folk art, culture, and history. Gibbon concluded his chapter on "Ukraine and Canada" with the text of the address of welcome to Lord Tweedsmuir on the occasion of his visit to Fraserwood, Manitoba, in 1936, and the governor-general's well-known reply.

Regardless of the evident tendency in the inter-war years to discuss Ukrainians in terms of their relevance to the question of assimilation or the "mosaic," an increasing number of works appeared, more narrowly concerned with their development and pertinent to Ukrainian-Canadian historiography.

Specific Studies and Research

The 1930s marked a turning point in English-language Ukrainian-Canadian historiography as serious scholarship and research into Ukrainain-Canadian development began to emerge from interested individuals or from academics within the university framework. Much of the literary activity in the decade immediately after the war had been of an exploratory nature, defining more precisely who the Ukrainians were, assessing their material and social progress after thirty years residence in the new land, and examining their folk culture with growing appreciation. Although interest in these areas persisted in Anglo-Saxon writings that dealt briefly or superficially with Ukrainians as one of many nationalities in Canada,[39] an increasing number of Anglo-Canadians came to recognize Ukrainian Canadians as a legitimate and significant collectivity whose development and history deserved careful scrutiny from various perspectives. Interest in Ukrainians was no longer confined to their influence and impact on Canadian national progress but also began to take into consideration their organizational and community life as being indicative of a self-contained and self-perpetuating subculture within the larger Canadian scene.

In 1931 the first monograph on Ukrainians was published. *The Ukrainian Canadians: A Study in Assimilation* by Charles H. Young was to constitute the sole general account of Ukrainian-Canadian history to be undertaken by an Anglo-Saxon, and despite its topical nature and dated perspective it remains one of the most important contributions to Ukrainian-Canadian historiography. Its insight into the question of assimilation from the Ukrainian point of view and its examination of Ukrainian-   45

Canadian society as a distinct and identifiable entity signalled a
new direction in the study of Ukrainians in Canada. Young's
research was sponsored by the Canadian National Committee for
Mental Hygiene on the premise that Canadian growth and
prosperity required citizens healthy in mind and body. It was felt
that such a study would enable one to determine the source of
potentially dangerous tendencies and suggest measures to
facilitate the mental adjustment of individual immigrants and
immigrant groups, thus circumventing the possibility of social
disorientation.[40] Ukrainians were selected for observation
because of their extensive distribution across Canada and
because their period of residence permitted an overview of the
effects of changed customs and environment on a succession of
generations.

To Young, Ukrainian Canadians were not to be studied outside
the context of their historical origins, but were to be seen as
progeny of Ukrainian parent groups. Unlike earlier Anglo-Saxon
writers, who had largely ignored or belittled the crystallizing
Ukrainian-Canadian community and observed Ukrainians
divorced from their organizational life (the exception being
occasional interest in their religious institutions), Young
recognized that this incipient society was the central factor
influencing Ukrainian-Canadian adjustment and the transition
between two worlds. Beginning with a concise and accurate
review of Ukrainian history,[41] he followed with a discussion of
Ukrainian immigration to Canada, dealing with rural and urban
patterns of settlement, agricultural and industrial development,
and the factors determining material success or failure. On a more
theoretical plane, he examined Ukrainian-Canadian society as a
self-contained unit and a distinct cultural entity, then considered
forces extraneous to that society — government, education, and
health — which were aggressively assimilative and prone to foster
social disorganization among the group. A final chapter assessed
Ukrainians in terms of their potential as Canadian citizens. That
Young's analysis took into account the influential role of the
community in the transitional process is less an indication of any
unique perceptiveness on his part than it is a reflection of a new
reality. The Ukrainian community grew increasingly vocal in its
demands during the inter-war period, and with a heightened
profile it became impossible for researchers into Ukrainian-
Canadian development to disregard the importance and existence
46 of that community.

Those chapters of *The Ukrainian Canadians* which examined immigration, settlement, distribution and expansion; rural colonies and agricultural progress; and urban ghettoes and industrial development; covered aspects of Ukrainian-Canadian life probed only superficially by Young's predecessors. His treatment of the subject was substantially more comprehensive, analytical, and objective; and his findings and conclusions formed the basis of future literature on these facets of Ukrainian-Canadian history for several years. In rural areas Young corroborated Woodsworth's findings of 1917 that economic and social progress was commensurate with the nature of the land settled, with Ukrainians making good on good land and showing less headway on poor land, especially in certain districts of Manitoba. One of the most outstanding features of Ukrainian agricultural progress was that it had been achieved with minimal financial assistance, guidance, or instruction from the Canadian government or private bodies. While earlier writers on Ukrainian urban life had focused on the first area of Ukrainian concentration — the inner-core slum, characterized by overcrowding, social unrest, and general decay — Young, in his discussion of the Winnipeg, Montreal, and Toronto Ukrainian communities, also noted the development of a second area of settlement beyond the original location. Viewing Ukrainian urban life not only from the standpoint of economic integration but also in terms of the development of both permanent and mobile Ukrainian-Canadian communities, he observed that Toronto and Montreal lay on the periphery of Ukrainian society and that Winnipeg was the organizational and institutional centre of the Ukrainian-Canadian world.

In both urban and rural Ukrainian settlements, Young confronted the question of assimilation and the ethnic bloc. Although retarding assimilation in rural districts, he argued that the ethnic ghetto was a valuable factor in an urban environment because it served to forestall too rapid assimilation and the subsequent social dislocation. Even the rural ethnic blocs were useful in that they provided a sense of community and social cohesion to offset the material discomfort entailed in the cultivation of marginal lands.

Young's examination of the various forces operating, interacting and conflicting within Ukrainian-Canadian society was a new departure in Ukrainian-Canadian historiography, for it attempted to explain attitudes, movements, and structures not so 47 much through Canadian stimuli as through European motivations and determinants. He concentrated on the religious and nationalistic affiliations and outlooks of the Ukrainian people in Canada, noting that identification with one group or another comprised their major social contacts. Although religious bodies had formed the nuclei of Ukrainian groups developing in Canada, their programs had expanded from a purely religious foundation to embrace also political, social, and cultural objectives as well. In many sectors of Ukrainian-Canadian society, nationalism was superseding older concerns. Organizations advocating self-help and self-expression were conceived by these religious and nationalist groups, eventually generating new attitudes and customs appropriate to Canadian life and furnishing a means of social control in the new land.

Young discerned two parallel tendencies operating in the Ukrainian-Canadian community. On the one hand, the formally organized groups and their representative institutions actively responded to political developments in the homeland, resulting in a pronounced nationalistic bias in their thinking and orientation. Without the agitation and propaganda conducted by the Ukrainian intelligentsia in Canada, Young doubted whether the latent nationalism among Ukrainian immigrants would have erupted as forcefully as it had, but he refused to view its manifestation negatively. Any drawback it posed for Canada through its perpetuation of European feuds and issues was counterbalanced by its role in giving birth to institutions useful as cohesive and unifying agents instrumental in alleviating social disorientation among Ukrainian immigrants. On the other hand, the major groups and their organizations were gradually assuming Canadian overtones and becoming increasingly concerned with easing the adjustment and integration of the Ukrainian people into Canadian life. In short, while the foundation of Ukrainian-Canadian society retained its Ukrainian roots, the superstructure would grow more Canadian. Behind Young's support of Ukrainian groups and institutions that were alien to Canadian society was the belief that Anglo-Canada could best approach Ukrainian immigrants on the basis of co-operation with their native institutions. Of secondary significance in their adaptation to Canadian life were the influences of non-indigenous institutions—government, educational, and medical — penetrating the Ukrainian-Canadian community.

48 Young agreed with his colleagues active in the issue of

immigration, that the best agent of assimilation was the public school. Although favouring the policy developed in Alberta, which had circumvented the problem of bilingual schools and teachers, he opposed neither the teaching of Ukrainian after hours (it helped to maintain a normal balance between Ukrainian parent and child) nor the employment of qualified Ukrainian teachers, arguing that given the qualifications demanded of every instructor, "the ideal teacher is one of the religion and race of the district."[42] Young claimed Ukrainians were no longer hostile to educational efforts by Canadian bodies, for their own leaders, concerned with the status of their group in Canada, were encouraging higher education; while the growing number of Ukrainians in institutions of higher learning bore testimony to their educational progress. Young concluded his discussion of the education of Ukrainian Canadians on this note:

Our attempt in this chapter has been to indicate trends and to evaluate the progress these people have made in the light of the circumstances under which they have lived. No picture of the situation is just or accurate which overlooks their handicaps or fails to note their great promise; with both of these in mind it must be admitted that they have done remarkably well.[43]

The Ukrainian Canadians appeared only two years after the publication of *The Central European Immigrant in Canada,* yet Young's attitude and assessment of educational developments among Ukrainians were markedly more sophisticated than those of Robert England.

Although critical of the unsatisfactory level of general health among Ukrainians, Young also took into consideration the physical and the psychological effects of living in an altered environment. Inadequate medical services in rural areas, fatalistic acceptance of illness, suffering, and death, and adherence to firmly-rooted traditions and superstitions in the healing of the sick all contributed to poor health. Enlistment of the co-operation of Ukrainian leaders, concerned as they were with elevating the status of their group, would certainly help any attempt to improve community health standards. In regards to Ukrainian relations with government institutions, Young examined their naturalization and political education as well as their movement into active participation in the political life of Canada through involvment in the administration of schools and   49 the municipal government. Unprepared as they were upon their arrival for participation in Canada's more democratic system of government, Ukrainians were rapidly acquiring sufficient knowledge of and interest in Canadian politics and the operation of government. Their willingness to co-operate with others in building the Canadian nation was a welcome sign, as their sheer numbers and concentration made them a potentially influential political force.

Lastly, to illustrate the degree of their assimilation, Young measured social disorder among Ukrainians in terms of the prevalence of different types of crime. He noted the universality of assault, petty thievery, destruction of property and lying, and the relative scarcity of serious offences, lawlessness, and sex crimes.[44] He also discussed factors conducive to an undue proportion of crime among Ukrainian immigrants and their children: an excessive number of males; ignorance of language, customs and laws; conflicts among their own factional groups; a magnified generation gap creating familial tensions; and the inconsistent and lax enforcement of the law. Temporary social disorganization and excessive criminality were the inevitable price one had to pay in the assimilation of non-Anglo-Saxon immigrant groups originating in a foreign cultural milieu. Simultaneously, however, Canadian organizations "longing for the chance to prove the quality of their citizenship" should deem it their national duty to implement programs designed to mitigate the social disorders and stress accompanying assimilation. Young concluded:

> While admitting the relatively high crime rate of the Ukrainians, our attempt . . . has been to show that such an excess of crime is to be expected in any immigrant group, and that it is even more to be expected among the Ukrainians, not through any innate racial propensity for crime but because of all the factors in the Ukrainian history, tradition and settlement in Canada which make for such social disorganization.[45]

Unlike his Anglo-Saxon predecessors concerned with the proclivity for crime manifested by Ukrainians in Canada, Young attempted to explain much of the phenomenon through the differences in attitudes, customs, and backgrounds.

In a final summary chapter, Young evaluated the suitability and desirability of Ukrainians as immigrants and prospective citizens, stating his own recommendations for their future immigration, colonization, and land settlement:

> The relative isolation of this group, as of most immigrant groups, owing to differences in culture, makes it difficult if not impossible for us to render them any but the most meagre of direct services. These at best should be of a sort to facilitate the work of the organizations germane to Ukrainian-Canadian society. The burden of their continuous development is one we can rarely share. Immigrant groups must, to a very great extent, work out their own salvation. And this we may rest assured the Ukrainians will do. No one can have intercourse with these more recent pioneers of our country, still more — know by personal experience their heroic efforts to meet the exacting tests of homesteading in the bush country on the North-west, without acquiring a feeling of confidence in their ability to measure up ultimately to the finest ideals of Canadian citizenship.[46]

In conducting his research, Young utilized a variety of sources — available statistics on different facets of Ukrainian-Canadian development, questionnaires that he distributed to hundreds of Ukrainians across Canada, a comparable program of interviews with Ukrainians from various backgrounds, and consultations with government officials, teachers, medical personnel, police officers, and others directly involved with the Ukrainian people of Canada. With only limited published material on Ukrainian Canadians on which to rely for authoritative information, this approach was essential for a meaningful study. In a balanced and relatively impartial investigation of Ukrainian-Canadian life, attitudes, assimilation, and the indigenous and alien forces at work within an immigrant society, Young displayed neither the prevailing Anglo-Saxon prejudices nor the predilection for one or another of the numerous Ukrainian groups that characterized much of the work of later Ukrainian writers. The interpretations of Ukrainian-Canadian history by Young's Ukrainian successors were often good examples of the partisanship and factionalism that he so astutely observed in the Ukrainian community.

Young's study was not only intended to depict the background, development, and progress of Ukrainians in Canada, but was to serve as a handbook for Canadian institutions and native-born Canadians active in the assimilation of Ukrainian immigrants and their children. Young's insight into immigrant psychology, adjustment, and assimilation (from the point of view of the immigrant) was remarkably enlightened when compared with the views of his predecessors writing on Ukrainian Canadians. He examined Ukrainians in Canada not in isolation or according to strictly Anglo-Canadian criteria—though these criteria were undoubtedly factors in his assessment of assimilation — but placed them within the context of their European background and their contemporary history. His approach to immigration and the problems it caused was decidedly sociological. Regardless of its topical limitations and restricted perspectives, Young's study still remains of unique value to Ukrainian-Canadian historiography because few Ukrainian-Canadian historians have examined pioneer Ukrainian development as a transition from old to new world patterns of behaviour, attitudes, and institutions. Young's orientation was thus much more influenced by the universality of certain phenomena among all immigrant groups; Ukrainian-Canadian writers have frequently confined their perspective to that of their own ethnic group.

The impact of *The Ukrainian Canadians* on literature pertaining to Ukrainian immigration, settlement, and development was immediately discernible. In 1936 Robert England published a second study, *The Colonization of Western Canada,* in which he evaluated the assimilation and contribution of the many European peoples inhabiting the prairie provinces in terms of the effect the economic depression of the 1930s was having on their agricultural development. After discussing the actual and potential contribution of several communities to the development of western Canada, England concluded that not only did they play a significant economic role, but that "it is to be hoped that in exploiting natural resources and in economic development some of the mother-wit, poetry, family affection, piety and wholesomeness of people bred to the soil will continue to enrich the life of the West."[47] As the chief organizer of the Community Progress Competitions for Continental Europeans, England also devoted considerable space to the successful realization of the project as a promotion of community and national consciousness and as a means for both preserving traditional handicraft skills and making continental Europeans more aware of available provincial health, agricultural, and educational services.

In opening his discussion of the Ukrainian element in western Canada, England admitted that they had been the most misunderstood racial group, but that recent studies outlining their history and background had helped to ameliorate the situation.[48] His subsequent heavy reliance on Young to indicate developments and progress in Ukrainian bloc settlements as well as factors in Ukrainian history bore testimony to the significance of *The Ukrainian Canadians* both as a source of information and a force in moulding attitudes more sympathetic to Ukrainians.[49] England stressed the marked improvements — social, cultural, educational, and economic — noticeable in Ukrainian communities in the last decade. It is interesting to note, however, that while in *The Central European Immigrant in Canada* he had stressed the role of the school as a community centre, he now referred to the popularity of social activities and gatherings of young people at community halls, perhaps an unconscious recognition of the success of the indigenous over the alien institution. England concluded his survey with the following remarks:

> There still remain some gaps in understanding as between the Ukrainian and Anglo-Saxon peoples. There has been a lack at times of neighborliness and a tendency to segregation of groups with consequent misunderstanding and a tendency to see one another in the blackest colors. There is a great deal of prejudice yet to be overcome and the work of reconciliation will be handicapped by the black sheep on each side. There is a form of myopia which attacks us when we can see our interests threatened by unusual modes of living or unaccustomed idioms or ways of thought, which at a distance would seem unattractive. The wider vision is ever the truer vision but detachment is not easy to achieve. We now know enough to realize the qualities which the best of the Ukrainian people have brought to Canada, and it is certain that when the history of Western Canada widens out in the coming decades there will be a high place on the scroll for the achievements of the Ukrainian people.[50]

Following Young's general account of Ukrainian-Canadian development, individuals in Canadian universities began to investigate specific issues or narrowly defined areas within the larger sphere of Ukrainian-Canadian life. However, before proceeding to those theses more valuable to Ukrainian-Canadian historiography, it is appropriate to summarize briefly those   53 works representing the culmination of Anglo-Saxon research into the education of Ukrainians in Canada.

As students of education became interested in Ukrainians, their first studies were typically utilitarian and unimaginative. In 1934 Claude H. Robinson submitted "A Study of the Written Language Errors of 1238 Pupils of Ukrainian Origin" to the University of Alberta as his B.Ed. thesis, proposing to ascertain the most frequently recurring types of error and thereby give teachers of Ukrainian pupils some indication of the points of construction to be emphasized. Robinson's study was notably amateurish and not based on any stated or tested standards. "A Study to Discover any Characteristic Differences in Sentence Structure in the Written English of Saskatchewan Elementary School Pupils Belonging to Different National Groups" was presented to the University of Saskatchewan in 1944 by Lorne H. Woollatt. It examined the types, frequency, and origin of errors in English sentence structure of pupils from English, German, Ukrainian, and French backgrounds. Woollatt found that different national groups made characteristic errors, suggesting the adoption of separate approaches in teaching them the English language. Unlike Robinson, he included a bibliography of related studies and pertinent literature and clearly defined his methods of classification, techniques for analyzing the data collected, and justification for accepting his results as reliable and valid.

To conclude our discussion of the literature concerned with teaching English to pupils of Ukrainian origin, a post-World War II thesis may be logically mentioned here. In 1946 David M. Sullivan wrote "An Investigation of the English Disabilities of Ukrainian and Polish Students in Grades IX, X, XI, XII of Alberta" for his M.Ed. degree. Gaining access to Alberta Department of Education files, he analyzed Grades IX and XII English examinations written by Ukrainian students in twenty-four selected schools, as well as the completed provincial Vocabulary, Comprehension, and Rate Tests for Grades X and XI. Of the three topically-related theses, Sullivan's was the most professional and mature study, acquiring its data and drawing its conclusions from undoubtedly the most uniform set of standards and types of material.

A thesis presented to the University of Toronto in 1941 by Jessie M. Deverell, "The Ukrainian Teacher as an Agent of Cultural Assimilation," investigated the extent and manner in which the growing numbers of Ukrainian teachers were

influencing the speed and smoothness of the assimilation of
Alberta Ukrainians. Deverell interviewed both Ukrainian and
non-Ukrainian teachers to obtain their views. On the assumption
that the Ukrainian teacher was better assimilated than his fellow
Ukrainians, she maintained that he was capable of acting as an
agent of assimilation in Ukrainian communities. However, her
interviewing also prompted her to conclude that only a small
minority of Ukrainian teachers consciously chose that profession
to assist in the assimilation of their people. After outlining the
merits and demerits of Ukrainian teachers as agents of cultural
assimilation, she closed on a positive note:

> A general summation of the results of this study would indicate
> that the Ukrainian teachers have had both accelerating and
> retarding influences on the speed with which the assimilation of
> their group has proceeded, but that they have definitely
> reduced the amount of friction attendant on the process. There
> seems to be little doubt that, in the natural process of time, the
> deterrent effects of their work will disappear, and that they will
> increasingly facilitate the complete fusion of the two cultures.[51]

A more substantial study examining the education of
Ukrainian Canadians, "Education in the Bloc Settlements of
Western Canada," was submitted by Leonard Bercuson to
McGill University in 1941. Concerned with the assimilation of the
foreign population of western Canada and the role of educational
institutions — past, present, and potential — in easing the
transition from one world to another, it echoed an oft-repeated
refrain in Anglo-Saxon literature on Ukrainians in Canada:

> The significance of the school and the teacher in the foreign
> colony cannot be overestimated. There is little doubt that
> education may well be the deciding factor in the crucial
> question of national unity. Western Canada requires schools
> and teachers of the finest type to take the lead in promoting the
> development of a national consciousness made up of the best
> elements in the diverse cultures which have been planted in our
> Dominion.[52]

Although Bercuson included all ethnic blocs in western Canada in
his discussion, he claimed intimacy only with the Ukrainian bloc
at Vegreville. Employed as a teacher at Smoky Lake for four
years, he travelled extensively in the summer months, inter-

55

viewing both Ukrainians and non-Ukrainians throughout the region. Those assimilative forces which Bercuson saw operating in the Ukrainian colony he assumed would also be at work among other nationalities, concluding that while rates might vary, assimilation would eventually triumph in all identifiable ethnic communities in western Canada. Bercuson consulted Young's *The Ukrainian Canadians* for general information on Ukrainian history, immigration, colonization, and organization. He maintained that in spite of their rural blocs, which had forestalled excessive social disorganization, thorough Canadianization of Ukrainians would be achieved within another generation.

The second section of Bercuson's thesis involved the psychology of assimilation, the teaching of bilingual children, and the role of education and the school in a community from the Canadian perspective and experience, but also taking into account different theories, experiments, and points of view on the part of educationalists throughout western civilization. Although related to the concrete situation in western Canada, Bercuson's thesis was considerably more theoretical and broadly based than were other similar studies on the education of Ukrainian Canadians.

Of more enduring value to the history of Ukrainians in Canada were three theses which examined isolated segments of Ukrainian-Canadian society. Two focused on the Ukrainian community in Montreal, while the third investigated the extensive Ukrainian bloc in northeastern Alberta. They all approached their subjects with the conviction that in each instance an identifiable Ukrainian-Canadian society existed and functioned in its own purposive manner. Any examination of the assimilation or adaptation to Canada of the Ukrainians in these areas necessarily had to be conducted through recognition and analysis of this fact.

In 1934 Stephen W. Mamchur submitted to McGill University his M.A. thesis, "The Economic and Social Adjustment of Slavic Immigrants in Canada: With Special Reference to the Ukrainians in Montreal." As previous writers had concentrated on rural Ukrainians, Mamchur felt the time ripe for similar treatment (but more sociological in emphasis) of urban Ukrainians. Positing that the amount of participation by an immigrant in Canadian life was determined by his spatial and occupational segregation, he argued that an analysis of the nature of segregation and development in regional and occupational distribution was imperative in measuring the adjustment of that immigrant group. Mamchur tested this contention with his case study of Ukrainians in Montreal, selected as typical of the peasant Slavic immigrant in the process of occupational and social adjustment in an urban environment. Being of Ukrainian origin himself, Mamchur was able to obtain personal entry into the Ukrainian immigrant milieu in Montreal and interviewed 11 per cent of the resident Ukrainian families, investigating employment, income, and expenditures. Mamchur was the first Ukrainian Canadian to produce an English-language study on a particular facet of Ukrainian-Canadian development; others would follow his initiative during the Second World War.

The second thesis to examine the Ukrainian community in Montreal was "The Social Structure of the Italian and Ukrainian Immigrant Communities in Montreal, 1935-1937." Written in 1939 by Charles M. Bayley, also at McGill University, it focused more on Italians than it did on Ukrainians but drew in both instances on comprehensive and intensive personal research. Bayley spent a total of twenty-two months visiting a cross-section of homes and organizations, and attending various social and religious functions within each community to get as complete and accurate a picture as possible. He described the nature and developmental patterns of Italian and Ukrainian settlements, dealing with such features as family life, trends, and changing roles; neighbourhood and institutional life at the core of the social structure of each community; and their forms of entertainment. He concluded:

> The outstanding result of the study has been an indication of how immigrants who came to Montreal in haphazard fashion without afore-considered planning or guidance, have moved in toward each other and adjusted as groups; of how they have developed a social life which is amazingly and highly satisfying; of how they find a place in relation to Canadian society and will continue to hold this station for some time. These facts cannot be overlooked in a consideration of the consequences of immigration.[53]

Bayley also claimed that despite the strength of Italian and Ukrainian corporate life — noting in particular the resilience of Ukrainians — adjustments in the social structures of both communities were inevitable. Any new immigration, however, would re-establish and revitalize the gradually eroding institutions and aid the perpetuation of alien languages, customs, and traditions. Bayley wrote prior to World War II, in whose aftermath large numbers of Ukrainian displaced persons arrived to augment and fortify Montreal's Ukrainian-Canadian community.

The third thesis was more historical than those by Mamchur and Bayley. "The Ukrainian Community in North Central Alberta" by Timothy C. Byrne was presented to the University of Alberta in 1937. Motivated by a fervent conviction of the necessity to assimilate Ukrainians, particularly in the light of the vigorous Ukrainian movement in Canada, Byrne emphasized both the problem and urgency of assimilation by focusing on the non-Canadian forces operating in Ukrainian-Canadian society.

Following a procedure almost universal among those who wrote on the history of Ukrainian Canadians, Byrne began with a sketch of Ukrainian historical development. Merely a skeleton, it contained no great factual errors.[54] He then surveyed the Ukrainian community in north central Alberta as to its geographical limits, settlement, poorer and better districts, division of centres and areas according to province of origin — Galicia or Bukovina, agricultural development, physical expansion until the depression, and urban centres. The core of his paper focused on the religious and secular divisions within the colony, and again Byrne attempted to establish a relationship between the province and village of origin of Ukrainians in different districts of Alberta, the dominant religious influences in these districts, and the relative popularity of different Ukrainian nationalist organizations. The source of Byrne's information lay in a summer's travels in the bloc, during which time he interviewed 150 Ukrainians regarding their financial status, political affiliations, history, and views on nationalism, assimilation, education, and marriage. When one considers that Byrne contacted only 150 out of the total 50,000 Ukrainians he claimed resided in the bloc, his methods and criteria for determining wealth, the statistical profile of the religious associations in various districts, and the popularity of the representative nationalist groups in different sections of the bloc, remain questionable.

The central concern of Byrne's study was to "indicate the ferment of ideas in a remote colony caused by the major dissensions among Ukrainians in Europe."[55] It remains a valuable description of the influence of rising Ukrainian nationalism in its many forms among Ukrainians in Canada from World War I into the 1930s, as viewed from an Anglo-Saxon perspective. That Byrne's attitude towards Ukrainian nationalism was less analytical than subjective is evident in his belief that in spite of the nationalists' contributions to Canada — and there were some — the realization of their aims would be disastrous for Canadian society, which above all required a unified national outlook. He declared:

> There is nothing more dangerous, nothing more detrimental to national progress than the spirit of "Little Ukrainianism." The eventual and complete fusion of the Ukrainian people with the other stocks that have settled in Western Canada is a social and political necessity.[56]

The Ukrainian bloc and nationalist movement had only served to impede assimilation.[57] It would have been preferable had the nationalist propaganda not stirred Ukrainian-Canadian society; Ukrainians would then have been naturally and quietly assimilated in time. At the same time Byrne doubted that the national movement would enjoy lasting success in Canada as the majority of Ukrainian Canadians were indifferent.

For the present, Ukrainian religious and secular organizations were doing little to promote the assimilation of their people.[58] Although the influence of the two Ukrainian churches was declining in the face of the increasing secularization of North American society, they continued to resist assimilation and actively fostered Ukrainian nationalism. Turning to the secular organization of Ukrainian-Canadian society, Byrne discussed three major nationalist groups — the Ukrainian Self-Reliance League, the National Union,[59] and the United Hetman Organization — in terms of their philosophies, orientations, aims, and objectives. He himself favoured the Ukrainian Self-Reliance League, Canadian in origin and lacking European connections, over the two other societies which he considered to be too foreign to Canada to provide leadership for Ukrainian Canadians. Although all three were dedicated to an independent Ukraine and equally professed loyalty to Canada, only the Ukrainian Self-Reliance League was concerned with the accommodation of the Ukrainian people to Canada, anxious to raise their cultural standards as a prelude to assimilation. Byrne concluded his study on an optimistic, if somewhat patronizing, note:

Ukrainians have proved themselves on the farm and in the classroom. They have passed through a trying period of initiation and have achieved the status of citizenship. They should be treated as fellow citizens. It is true that there are aberrations within Ukrainian society that are unhealthy to Canadian interests. But these aberrations are not so serious that they cannot be corrected by a helping hand and a square deal. Tolerance is a crying need in the treatment of our Ukrainian Canadians.[60]

While Mamchur's thesis in 1934 had inaugurated English-language study of Ukrainians in Canada by Ukrainians themselves, their first publications did not appear until the war years. The two most enduring works were *Canadian Cossacks* by William Paluk, and *Canadians of Ukrainian Origin: Population* by Nicholas J. Hunchak. A collection of essays, articles and short stories on Ukrainian-Canadian life, the former was published in 1943, much of it having been printed previously in the *Canadian Ukrainian Review,* a Ukrainian war veterans' magazine of which Paluk was a contributing editor. Simply written, Paluk's material was not directed towards a learned or cultured audience but intended for popular consumption. *Canadian Cossacks* contained considerable information on Ukrainian background, development, and characteristics as well as Ukrainian life in Canada, but was highly impressionistic and superficial and tinged with nostalgia. It therefore did little to advance the study of Ukrainian Canadians.

Of greater historical value was Hunchak's *Canadians of Ukrainian Origin: Population.* It was intended to be the introductory volume in a series of statistical studies on Ukrainians in Canada published by the newly-formed Ukrainian Canadian Committee but, unfortunately, further issues failed to materialize. Utilizing the Dominion Bureau of Statistics census returns for 1941, Hunchak's work was strictly a compilation of population figures on a national and provincial scale and according to several classifications: numerical importance, religious denominations, occupations, birthplace, immigration, citizenship, official language and mother tongue, conjugal condition, age, and education. It also indicated the numbers of Ukrainians in those municipalities, cities, towns, and villages in which they resided, with similar information on those of

Austrian, Polish, Romanian, and Russian origin on the

assumption that Ukrainians were often erroneously included among them. *Canadians of Ukrainian Origin: Population* was primarily a source book useful to those interested in analysing the statistical data assembled by Hunchak, as he himself did not interpret the figures he presented.

In contrast to the situation in World War I, when Ukrainians received scant attention in contemporary literature, despite the fact that they were classified as enemy aliens, the years of World War II witnessed the publication of a considerable amount of material pertaining to Ukrainians and the war. Anglo-Canadians with various motives attempted to illustrate the loyalty of Ukrainian Canadians to the Allied war effort and the Canadian nation. Those concerned with national unity, both as it affected Canada's performance in the current conflict and a program for post-war national reconstruction, discussed the different national groups in Canada within this context. In a sense, these combined writings marked a peak in Anglo-Canadian literary interest in the development of Ukrainians and their role in the creation of a Canadian identity. Examination of Ukrainian Canadians by non-Ukrainians would continue on a drastically reduced scale; in the decades following 1945 the balance of such work would be done by Ukrainian Canadians themselves. Other war-time writings worth mentioning were the numerous declarations of Ukrainian-Canadian support for the Allied cause.

The most prolific Anglo-Saxon exponent of Ukrainian-Canadian loyalty was Watson Kirkconnell, a noted linguist, scholar, and patron of Ukrainians.[61] In his World War II writings, he studied Ukrainian Canadians, as well as other ethnic groups, in terms of their attitudes towards Canada, her allies, and the Axis powers. Kirkconnell's first publication, *Canada, Europe, and Hitler*, in 1939 sought to clarify the national and international issues facing the Dominion in the wake of the menace of Hitler and Nazism. He obtained his data from an extensive examination of the views expressed in the ethnic press on the eve of the war and in the light of developments in the mother countries of central and eastern Europe.[62] His task was complicated by the fact that many of the national groups were split into discordant factions. The most politically self-conscious of Canada's minorities, Ukrainian Canadians were divided not only into antagonistic nationalist and communist camps, but also into hostile nationalist factions. Through scrutiny of their representative newspapers, Kirkconnell   61 analysed in turn their attitudes towards Nazi Germany, their reactions to the creation of a Ukrainian state in Trans-Carpathia, and their opinions on the Allied associations with Poland and Russia. From his observation that each national group recognized the Nazi threat to world security, Kirkconnell concluded that resistance to its expansion would provide a common purpose and unity to all Canadians.[63]

Kirkconnell also wrote two pamphlets devoted exclusively to Ukrainian Canadians and their attitudes towards the war. The first, published in 1940 under the title *The Ukrainian Canadians and the War,* emphasized Ukrainian loyalty to Canada in her struggle overseas. Kirkconnell summarized his purpose as follows:

> This was an attempt to set forth the war aims of Canada and Britain in terms which would appeal to the loyalties of the Ukrainian Canadians both as Ukrainians and as Canadians, and would encourage them to sink their differences in a common Canadian war effort. Incidentally, I again stressed the idea that a Ukrainian sovereign state in Europe might well be an anachronism hopelessly late for a time when large European federations were needed for the peace and welfare of the continent.[64]

The second pamphlet, *Our Ukrainian Loyalists: The Ukrainian Canadian Committee,* was originally an address delivered in 1943 to the First All-Canadian Congress of Ukrainians in Canada. It was a defence of the loyalist non-communist Ukrainians as represented by the Ukrainian Canadian Committee against slanderous attacks by the ostracized communist sector of the community.[65] Kirkconnell outlined the steps in the formation of the Ukrainian Canadian Committee, enumerating its aims and objectives along with an account of his role in its creation in an attempt to vindicate himself from charges perpetrated against him. He also discussed the inter-war political organizations and alignments of Ukrainian Canadians and their present war record. He was highly critical of the communist Ukrainian Labor-Farmer Temple Association (ULFTA) and its "anti-Canadian" political education.

Much of Kirkconnell's energy in *Our Ukrainian Loyalists* was directed towards refuting charges made against him in a book by

Raymond A. Davies, *This is Our Land: Ukrainian Canadians*

Against Hitler, published in 1943. Written from the Ukrainian communist point of view, it was a popular, propagandistic book designed to exonerate the outlawed ULFTA by depicting the organization as an anti-fascist exponent of Canada's Soviet allies, with a membership that was loyal to the Canadian war effort.[66] At the same time Davies endeavoured to expose non-communist Ukrainian organizations, particularly the monarchist United Hetman Organization and the fascist Ukrainian National Federation (both traditionally anti-Soviet), as the true villains in the Ukrainian-Canadian community.[67] He decried the error of the Canadian government in supporting these nationalist groups over the suppressed and ill-treated ULFTA, but in his attempt to provide evidence of the support of the ULFTA membership to Canada and the Allied cause, he conveniently ignored the years of the Soviet-German pact and began his discussion with the German invasion of the Soviet Union. Davies also provided a condensed résumé of Ukrainian-Canadian history in which his communist bias generated an erroneous impression of the relative significance of the different political organizations in Ukrainian-Canadian society, and the political orientation of the majority of Ukrainian Canadians. This section implied that most Ukrainian Canadians, represented by the ULFTA until its suppression, were sympathetic to the Ukrainian Soviet Republic, and that the Ukrainian National Federation and United Hetman Organization were minor and disruptive forces within the community.

In that literature concerned primarily with Canadian unity during the war years and the period of reconstruction, Ukrainians were usually discussed as simply one of many national groups within Canada's borders.[68] A pamphlet written by Kirkconnell in 1941 under the authority of the Minister of National War Services and entitled *Canadians All: A Primer of Canadian National Unity,* outlined a policy for Canada to adopt towards the "permanent unification of all our groups into one strong, resolute nation," an important undertaking as the many races and creeds provided fertile ground for Nazi underground infiltration. Attacking both the Nazis and the Communists, Kirkconnell contended that they were least successful when recruiting among European Canadians, who were well aware of the true natures of their totalitarian ideologies. He claimed that the vast majority of Ukrainian Canadians had buried their differences for the sake of the Canadian war effort and were among those unmoved by Nazi or Soviet Propaganda.

Frances Swyripa

Ukrainian Canadians had for some time published booklets in their native tongue outlining the development and aspirations of their different organizations. Wartime spokesmen for the community reiterated their loyalty to Canadian ideals in Ukrainian-language publications, but the war years also witnessed the adoption of English (initially on a minor scale) to publicize Ukrainian solidarity with fellow Canadians in the task confronting the nation. For instance, in 1943 the Ukrainian National Federation published a pamphlet, *A Program and a Record,* primarily to preserve a record of its objectives and activities during the first decade of its existence, but also to note the organization's reaction to the outbreak of war. Although the booklet focused on Canadian concerns and stressed Ukrainian dedication to the defence of Canada, it also defended the Ukrainian National Federation against attacks and allegations by the Communists and denied the organization had European affiliations. A second pamphlet, *Canadians on the March,* was the text of a series of radio broadcasts presented in 1944 by the Ukrainian Canadian Cultural Group in Yorkton, Saskatchewan. The broadcasts were intended to spur Ukrainian Canadians into serving Canada by fostering a pride in their past. Although superficial and redundant, *Canadians on the March* contained remarks from numerous delegates to the First All-Canadian Congress of Ukrainians in Canada, providing contemporary personal impressions of an enthusiastic response to the creation of the Ukrainian Canadian Committee and its objectives. It also aired views on the Ukrainian Canadian's obligations to Canada, passionately espousing the necessity of loyalty and good citizenship.

It was between 1939 and 1945 that Ukrainian Canadians themselves began to assume the function of English-language spokesmen for their group. Initially their works were mostly topical, dealing with such issues as the Ukrainian situation in Europe and the need for Ukrainian Canadians to support the Allied cause, rather than attempting to study scientifically the history of the group in Canada. In the following years Ukrainian Canadians, both the native-born and the post-war immigrants, supplanted non-Ukrainians in the field of Ukrainian-Canadian research, and Ukrainian-Canadian historiography in the English language became a recognizable discipline.

A Maturing Discipline

Since World War II, research into Ukrainian-Canadian development has been conducted from historical, sociological, demographic, and philological perspectives. Although non-Ukrainians have occasionally selected the Ukrainian group in Canada for examination in relation to their discipline, the bulk of the research and writing on Ukrainians has been done by Ukrainian Canadians themselves. Much of this activity stems from the fact that as Canadian-born Ukrainians began to enter university they often developed an interest in their own background which led to their investigation of various aspects of Ukrainian life. Another factor that encouraged the study of Ukrainians in Canada was the arrival of Ukrainian intellectuals with the migration of displaced persons to Canada after 1948. Although handicapped professionally by their inability to speak English, the post-war immigrants were highly instrumental in the scholarly organization of the Ukrainian-Canadian community, establishing Canadian branches of the Ukrainian Free Academy of Sciences and the Shevchenko Scientific Society. This period also saw the introduction of Ukrainian courses at Canadian universities. With the Ukrainian-Canadian community now organized intellectually as well as religiously and secularly, it is not surprising that research into Ukrainian-Canadian history flourished.

As the quantity of English-language literature on Ukrainian Canadians has multiplied in the last three decades, it has been necessary to introduce a process of selection — as unjust or arbitrary as it might sometimes seem to be — in this final chapter of our study. What is proposed is a thoroughgoing treatment of published monographs and theses pertinent to Ukrainian-Canadian history and of those articles that express an explicit point of view or argument in their interpretation of the role of   65

Ukrainian Canadians in the development of Canada or the Ukrainian-Canadian community.

The communist sector of the Ukrainian-Canadian community has been traditionally ostracized by the nationalist majority and as a consequence its historical role in Ukrainian-Canadian development has been largely ignored or detrimentally distorted in the writings of nationalist Ukrainian Canadians. The first published monograph on Ukrainian Canadians by a member of the community, however, was written from the Ukrainian communist point of view. *Men in Sheepskin Coats: A Study in Assimilation* by Vera Lysenko was also compromised by its political bias, but was partially redeemed by its valuable insights into the nature and plight of the non-agricultural Ukrainian immigrant. Usually a single male transient labourer with a peculiar life style and unique problems, the immigrant worker was a distinct phenomenon in the early history of Ukrainians in Canada. For many years Ukrainian-Canadian writers relegated this phase of Ukrainian experience in Canada to the background, overshadowed as it was by the predominance of the immigrant agriculturalist.[1]

The first section of *Men in Sheepskin Coats* dealt with the history of Ukrainian immigration and subsequent development in the new country; the second, "They Came from Cossack Land," looked at the historical background and traditions of the Ukrainian people, portrayed in a somewhat romantic vein; and the third section examined the assimilation of Ukrainians into Canadian life at various levels. While Lysenko revealed admirable insight into the psychology of assimilation and the reactions of successive generations of Ukrainian Canadians to both their Ukrainian and Canadian heritages, her political orientation contributed to a deliberate misinterpretation of certain phenomena in Ukrainian and Ukrainian-Canadian development and to a misplaced emphasis on individual movements and events. An often popular and pseudo-novelistic style and the absence of footnotes — despite an extensive bibliography — have also undermined the scholarly quality of *Men in Sheepskin Coats*.

Lysenko's emphasis on the Ukrainian labourer to the exclusion of the agriculturist was undoubtedly prompted by her marxist concern for the industrial proletariat, but to the unsuspecting reader it could inaccurately suggest that the majority of

Ukrainian-Canadians were urbanized workers. More damaging

yet to the credibility of Lysenko's study was her account of the religious structures and divisions in Ukrainian-Canadian society. She provided a lengthy review of the establishment and fortunes of the Independent Greek Church and devoted considerable space to East Ukrainian Stundists or Baptists, a group who emigrated to Canada in small numbers from the Russian Empire under similar conditions as had the Doukhobors. Lysenko concluded that while Stundism had answered "deep needs of life in the world of the Ukrainian peasant" in its opposition to religious corruption and political and economic oppression, the Independent Greek movement had been imposed from the outside and identified with the Anglo-Saxon program of assimilation. In contrast to her treatment of the Independent Greek Church and Stundism, Lysenko dismissed the growth of the Greek Catholic Church in Canada in one paragraph. She stated that "gradually the influence of this church, pursuing an aggressive policy to win converts, became the dominant religious power among Ukrainians in Canada,"[2] completely ignoring its role in Galicia as a Ukrainian national institution and the fact that the majority of the Ukrainian immigrants who came to Canada were raised as Greek Catholics. Lastly, Lysenko ignored the establishment of the Ukrainian Greek Orthodox Church of Canada altogether, again undermining the authority and value of her study.

The final area of gross misrepresentation in Lysenko's characterization of Ukrainian-Canadian society involved her depiction of community organization. Lysenko elevated the communist Ukrainian Labor-Farmer Temple Association (ULFTA) and its successor, the Association of United Ukrainian Canadians (AUUC), to a dominant position in the life of Ukrainian Canadians and intimated that the vast majority were sympathetic to the present Soviet Ukrainian state and its Russian overlord. Although her emphasis implied that all those touched by the organization shared its political philosophy, Lysenko cannot be blanketly condemned for her evaluation of the role of the ULFTA in Ukrainian-Canadian life. Charles Young had contended that during the Great Depression of the 1930s, the ULFTA was the only Ukrainian organization to respond to the immediate economic and social needs of Ukrainian-Canadians, and hence was more influential than the actual numbers of its political adherents would suggest.[3]

In her discussion of the impact of the events of 1917 to 1923 on 67

Ukrainians in Canada, Lysenko's communist bias became
glaringly apparent. She completely disregarded the Ukrainian
national movement and revolution, dealing only with the
establishment of a communist government in Kharkiv, and
lauding the formation of the Soviet Ukraine:

> The establishment of a Soviet Ukrainian state made possible
> the development of Ukraine's economy, her political life and
> cultural institutions on a scale not possible during the centuries
> of national oblivion when the Ukraine was enslaved in that
> "prison-house of peoples," the tsarist regime. . . . By 1937 the
> country was completely industrialized, with hundreds of large
> factories, giant steel and metallurgical plants, machine-
> building shops, mining and hydro-electric industries were
> developed, and the whole agricultural economy was
> reconstructed on a Socialist basis. The development in
> education made similar gigantic strides: from a pre-tsarist
> figure of 19 higher educational institutions with 20,000
> students, the number had risen by 1939 to 121 institutions with
> 122,000 students; public schools, kindergartens, libraries and
> research institutes increased proportionately. The magnitude
> of changes going on in their native land naturally had marked
> repercussions among the Ukrainian immigrants in Canada.
> Previous to the war, there were Socialist groups, but these had
> no mass appeal because they lacked direction and purpose.
> With the growth of the new Ukrainian state, however, a large
> body of Ukrainian Canadians responded sympathetically to
> the efforts of the Soviet Republic to develop its national life.
> There occurred at this period a division of thought among the
> Ukrainians in Canada: one group, as has been described,
> consisting largely of members of the Ukrainian Labor-Farmer
> Temple Association, regarded with admiration and approval
> the achievements of the new Ukrainian state; another group,
> now calling themselves nationalists, opposed the changes
> bitterly, refusing to recognize the Soviet Ukrainian State.[4]

Lysenko then proceeded to sketch the development of the
socialist sector of the Ukrainian-Canadian community. She failed
to discuss the nationalist organizations except to note the
antagonism between the inter-war Ukrainian immigrant intellectual who was often uncomfortable in the changed milieu and still
oriented to Old World politics, and the pioneering peasant who

had earned his station in Canadian society "by the sweat of his brow" and without the leadership of an educated elite. Another serious omission that betrayed Lysenko's partisanship was her refusal to even acknowledge the existence of the Ukrainian Canadian Committee, claimed by anti-communist Ukrainian Canadians to be the highlight in community organization.[5]

Similarly, in her interpretation of the Ukrainian historical experience, Lysenko revealed her socialist perspective despite the fact that she concentrated on Ukrainian traditions, characteristics, and folk culture. Lysenko's emphasis on the Cossack heritage and its romantic image was rather misleading, as the majority of the Ukrainians in the first two immigrations were not the "descendents of the Cossacks" but from Western Ukraine, historically peripheral to Cossackdom. In her assessment of both Bohdan Khmelnytsky, leader of the 1648 Revolution against Poland, and of Ivan Mazepa, the hetman who challenged Peter I of Russia and met with defeat at the Battle of Poltava in 1709, Lysenko adopted the official Soviet view. Thus, Khmelnytsky was the "founder of firm union between Russia and Ukraine" while Mazepa was

> ... an adventurer who might have, if he had chosen to strengthen the union with Russia that Bohdan began so auspiciously assured for the Ukraine an honorable place among the nations of Europe; but instead Mazepa chose to align himself against the victorious Peter the Great — and thus lost a country for himself and a happy future for his people.[6]

In the final section of *Men in Sheepskin Coats,* Lysenko discussed the Canadianization of Ukrainians in Canada. "Now at last, the pattern for assimilation is beginning to emerge, revealing itself, not as conformity, but as unity in diversity, enabling the immigrant, with his physical hardihood, artistry and deep sources of originality, to enter into the innumerable facets of national life."[7] She depicted the process of assimilation in representative spheres — organized life, community interaction, family life with its inevitable tensions between generations — all leading to the achievement of a balanced social order and material and spiritual success. The tendency to cite individual success stories as proof of Ukrainian progress, vertical mobility, and integration, later to become an almost universal approach among Ukrainian-Canadian historians, was already evident in *Men in Sheepskin*   69

Coats. Lysenko highlighted the cultivation of Ukrainian folk arts in the contemporary daily life of Ukrainian Canadians, but also noted changes made under the influence of the Canadian environment and the development of a certain artificiality as the spontaneity of the original cultural milieu was lost and many customs became anachronistic in the modern industrial world. At times she spoke on the personal level of the psychological problems of adjustment she faced with others of her generation, who were forced to confront, as children of immigrants, the reconciliation of old and new values. She observed that within the younger generation, however, conflicts were diminishing and assimilation was triumphing. The solidarity developed among Canadians of all origins during World War II had continued in the post-war years, and in this atmosphere Ukrainian Canadians had become fully integrated into Canadian life until "the youngest generation belonged wholly to the New World."[8]

Obviously, *Men in Sheepskin Coats* was not an objective or balanced account of Ukrainian-Canadian history. Yet despite its inaccuracies and overemphasis on the size and role of the communist segment within Ukrainian-Canadian society, it was a refreshing addition to Ukrainian-Canadian historiography in the light of the neglect of the left-wing elements by writers in the nationalist camp. Lysenko's pro-Soviet stance — as misleading as it was in its suggestion that the majority of Ukrainian Canadians held a similar opinion — was informative and valuable as an expression of a point of view seldom encountered in Ukrainian-Canadian histories. *Men in Sheepskin Coats* was to remain the only major account of Ukrainian-Canadian history to be written in English from the perspective of a communist Ukrainian Canadian, until very recently.

As Ukrainians in Canadian universities began to select topics in Ukrainian-Canadian history as subjects for theses and dissertations, they chose specific areas of the community's development for examination. The first thesis produced in this vein was Paul Yuzyk's initial contribution to Ukrainian-Canadian historical scholarship, an M.A. thesis submitted to the University of Saskatchewan in 1948 entitled "The History of the Ukrainian Greek Catholic (Uniate) Church in Canada." Exploring new territory, it constituted the first serious and documented study of the growth of this primary Ukrainian-Canadian religious institution.[9] Basically a factual, chronological narration of its

Canadian development, structure and activities, it also discussed the organization and history of the Ukrainian Greek Catholic Church in Europe as a necessary condition of any complete understanding of the movement in Canada. Yuzyk concluded that thirty-five years after its incorporation the Canadian church was remarkably well-developed but since 1931 had been confronted with a decreasing number of adherents, the result of inherent weaknesses within the church structure and trends within Canadian society. Yuzyk suggested that its survival required both internal analysis and adjustments to Canadian society.

Although chronologically out of place at this point in our discussion, Yuzyk's doctoral dissertation, "Ukrainian Greek Orthodox Church of Canada (1918-1951)," presented to the University of Minnesota in 1958, complemented his prior study on the Greek Catholic Church in Canada. Also a pioneer work on the rise of the Ukrainian Greek Orthodox Church of Canada under the initiative of an émigré nationalist petty intelligentsia,[10] it dealt with the church's difficulties in obtaining recognition from the Orthodox world, and covered its genesis, growth, and eventual stabilization, in an essentially factual manner. Although neither thesis contained much in the way of interpretation, the tone of his second work was more positive, although retaining objectivity and showing evidence of thorough research. Yuzyk's works are still considered to be the basic English-language studies of the history of the traditional Ukrainian churches. Other theses, however, have examined specific areas of interest in the activities of the two churches, notably their role in education.

The first to appear, "The Ukrainian Settlers in Canada and their Schools with Reference to Government, French-Canadian, and Ukrainian Missionary Influences 1891-1921," was presented to the University of Alberta in 1958 by the Reverend John Skwarok, OSBM, for his M.Ed. degree. The purpose of his study was "to determine what steps were taken to meet a growing challenge in education during the pioneering life of the Ukrainian settlers and wherever possible to evaluate the effectiveness of the procedures adopted."[11] By focusing on the work of French and Ukrainian Catholic missionaries and secular Ukrainian teachers, however, and ignoring the influence of Anglo-Saxon pedagogues and the sincere efforts of the prairie governments (apart from their operation of Ruthenian Training Schools), Skwarok presented as incomplete and misleading an account of the subject as had the early Anglo-Saxon observers writing on the education 71 of immigrant Ukrainians. Skwarok's paper was characterized by its paucity of analysis, its Ukrainian-Catholic bias and its occasionally emotional tone; it was primarily a summary and factual record, coupled with praise, of the educational work of Ukrainian and French-Canadian missionaries, and Ukrainian instructors and training schools.

"The Ukrainian Settlers in Canada and their Schools" was a poorly written and disjointed work that lacked a synthesizing overview and had a tendency to drift into irrelevancy.[12] In some instances its author was mistaken in his facts, while at other times he was plagued by careless editing.[13] All too typically, Skwarok intimated that Poland existed as an independent country prior to 1914[14] and he then exaggerated the peasant's awareness of his Ukrainianness, claiming him to be "intensely conscious of his national identity."[15] In his attempt to paint as black a picture as possible of the plight of the Ukrainian peasantry, and thereby justify the motivation behind their migration to Canada, Skwarok maintained that they were forbidden to speak Ukrainian in their native land,[16] which was never true in Galicia. Even in the Russian Empire, where the Valuyev Ukaz (1863) and the Ukaz of Ems (1876) had forbidden publications in the Ukrainian language, peasants had never been forced to converse in Russian, and, following the 1905 Revolution, restrictions on the written use of Ukrainian were also lifted. In describing conditions under which the Ukrainian peasantry lived in the Austrian Empire, Skwarok failed to clarify the situation as it had developed from the Josephinian reforms at the end of the eighteenth century, through the abolition of serfdom in 1848.[17] His confused account only served to misinform unknowing Anglo-Canadian writers as to the situation of Galician-Ukrainian peasants at the time of their emigration.[18]

The second thesis to examine a traditional Ukrainian church and its role in education, "A Historical Study of the Development of the Ukrainian Greek Orthodox Church of Canada and its Role in the Field of Education (1918-1964)," was written in 1965 for the University of Manitoba by Odarka S. Trosky, the daughter of a Ukrainian Orthodox priest. It considered the development and activities of the Ukrainian Orthodox institutes in Saskatoon, Edmonton, and Toronto, and of the various lay organizations promoting education among the church's membership. By education Trosky meant not only the academic training undertaken by the institutes, but religious, Ukrainian national, political, and cultural instruction as well. The major portion of her thesis involved a detailed discussion of the creation, the difficult years, and the eventual consolidation and entrenchment of the Ukrainian Greek Orthodox Church of Canada: in this respect it paralleled Yuzyk's earlier study.

Trosky, however, like Skwarok, was innaccurate in her description of conditions in Galicia at the turn of the century: "The existence of Ukrainians as a separate ethnic group was denied, learning of Ukrainian language and development of Ukrainian culture was not permitted and political organizations were suppressed."[19] She related Canadian democracy and freedom of conscience and association with the rise of a Ukrainian Greek Orthodox Church in Canada based on similar ideological principles. Written as it was with admitted Orthodox sympathies and praise for the accomplishments of that institution during the first fifty years of its existence, Trosky's work contained no objective and historical evaluation of the emergence, development, and achievements of the Ukrainian Greek Orthodox Church of Canada. This is not surprising when one considers that her bibliography was almost exclusively comprised of Ukrainian Orthodox publications.

One other thesis has examined the religious life of Ukrainian Canadians. In 1959 Murray Wenstob submitted to the University of Alberta, his B.D. thesis entitled "The Work of the Methodist Church among Settlers in Alberta up to 1914, with Special Reference to the Formation of Congregations and Work among the Ukrainian People." He clearly endorsed the activities of the Methodist Church in his admiring description of the many accomplishments of the Methodist missionaries, societies, medical personnel, and lay people working with Ukrainians at Pakan, Lamont, Wahstao, and Kolokreeka, in Edmonton, and among miners at Blairmore.[20] Quoting extensively from letters published in the Methodist *Missionary Bulletin,* Wenstob did not present a balanced or analytical investigation of Methodist missions among Ukrainian immigrants in Alberta, but did assess the methods and results of their work from a Methodist point of view.

He claimed that Methodist representatives had facilitated the adjustment of Ukrainians to Canadian life by establishing hospitals and schools in addition to promoting religious enlightenment. A poor command of the Ukrainian language and unfamiliarity with Ukrainian customs and culture, however, had   73 hampered the missionaries in their work. Wenstob concluded:

> Although the statistics of the Galician work do not show a marked success I am convinced that the success is showing up now in the second and third generations of Galicians. We need only to look at the United Church rolls of members and adherents to see the many Ukrainian names; names of families which came to Canada as Greek Catholics.[21]

Whether or not the increase in the number of Ukrainian adherents of the United Church of Canada can be attributed to the early missionary work of the Methodist and Presbyterian churches remains debatable. Equally significant have been such factors as intermarriage,[22] the loss of the Ukrainian language — so vital to the practice of the Ukrainian Catholic and Ukrainian Orthodox faiths—and increased secularization and Canadianization.

In 1952 Harry Piniuta submitted to the University of Ottawa the first thesis by a Ukrainian Canadian to concentrate specifically on a secular Ukrainian organization. "The Organizational Life of Ukrainian Canadians; with Special Reference to the Ukrainian Canadian Committee," briefly surveyed the various political and religious groups within the Ukrainian community in Canada, then focused on the formation of the Ukrainian Canadian Committee, describing its achievements and role in contemporary Canadian life. The introductory section on Ukrainian immigration and settlement contained a number of inexcusable factual errors. For example, Piniuta referred to Josef Oleskiw as "Nicholas" and incorrectly dated his Canadian tour as 1888 instead of 1895. He also mistakenly referred to John M. Gibbon as "George."[23] The organizational development of Ukrainian Canadians was inadequately presented in skeletal form, and Piniuta's biases towards the different groups were thinly veiled. He concluded that while the Ukrainian Canadian Committee had justified its creation, it was still needed to counteract the persistent communist menace and the lingering barriers of prejudice. A pioneer work on a particular aspect of Ukrainian-Canadian history, Piniuta's unsatisfactory treatment of the subject has since been surpassed by other studies dealing with the formation and activities of the Ukrainian Canadian Committee.

74 Research into the teaching of English to Ukrainian pupils and

the role of the school and the teacher in Canadianization —
initially conducted by Anglo-Canadians — was taken up in the
post-1945 era by Ukrainian Canadians working in the field. "An
Analysis of English Errors and Difficulties among Grade Ten
Students in the Smoky Lake School Division" by Michael Skuba
was presented to the University of Alberta for an M.Ed. degree in
1955. Using data obtained from the results of a standard
American English examination, Skuba attempted to determine
those qualities of the English language most difficult for
Ukrainian students to grasp, concluding that sixty to eighty per
cent of the grade ten students of Ukrainian origin in the Smoky
Lake School Division were below the norms for their grade. In
1966 Alec Saruk submitted to the University of Alberta his M.Ed.
thesis on the "Academic Performance of Students of Ukrainian
Descent and the Cultural Orientation of their Parents." Initially
postulating that the academic performance of students whose
parents were bilingual or English-oriented would exceed that of
those from Ukrainian-oriented or apathetic backgrounds, Saruk
was forced to conclude that no such relationship could be traced
in the fourteen schools in northeastern Alberta where he
compared the results of grade IX departmental examinations for
1963 and 1964, with data obtained from an acculturation survey
taken among grade X and XI students. A similar paper, "Cultural
Orientation of Rural Ukrainian High School Students," was
presented to the University of Calgary in 1969 by M.Ed.
candidate Carolyn R. Harasym. Lastly, in 1968, a University of
Saskatchewan student named Sonia V. Cipywnyk prepared a
voluminous study entitled "Educational Implications of
Ukrainian-English Childhood Bilingualism in Saskatchewan,"
also for an M.Ed. degree.

"Lexical Borrowings in Alberta Ukrainian," written at the
University of Alberta in 1965 by Alexander Royick, focused on
the use of borrowed English words that were either direct
incorporations or hybrid derivatives — especially in verb forms
and diminutive nouns — in the language of immigrant
Ukrainians. It also examined dialectical borrowings from
continental languages — Polish, Russian, Romanian, and Czech
— with which Ukrainians came into contact in Europe. Apart
from its value to students to the Ukrainian language, "Lexical
Borrowings in Alberta Ukrainian" geographically locates the
various Ukrainian dialects in Alberta and thus helps to determine
the village or district of origin of many Alberta Ukrainians. It

revealingly documents the linguistic transformation of the Ukrainian language in the Anglophone environment of Canada.[24]

During the 1950s, two of the most outstanding students of Ukrainian-Canadian history began to publish the results of their research. In this decade, Paul Yuzyk made a significant contribution to Ukrainian-Canadian historiography with publication of *The Ukrainians in Manitoba: A Social History,* while Vladimir J. Kaye-Kysilewskyj — eventually to become one of the most meticulous researchers into Ukrainian-Canadian development — published some relevant material on a less ambitious scale.

In a pamphlet written in 1951—*Slavic Groups in Canada*—Kaye discussed the Ukrainian and Polish communities beginning with a lengthy introduction outlining the adjustment pattern of immigrant ethnic groups and their gradual absorption into Canadian life. To illustrate the integration of Ukrainian Canadians into the various spheres of Canadian life—social, economic (principally in agriculture), and political—he enumerated numerous individual success stories. A second article by Kaye, "The Ukrainians in Canada," appeared in a book edited by John A. Kosa, a collection of lectures on Canadian immigration delivered in Montreal in 1954 and published under the title *Immigrants in Canada.* It basically reiterated the material contained in *Slavic Groups in Canada.*[25]

One of the primary studies in Ukrainian-Canadian history has been Paul Yuzyk's treatise, *The Ukrainians in Manitoba: A Social History,* published in 1953 as the first in a series of ethnic studies sponsored by the Historical and Scientific Society of Manitoba. The numerical strength of Ukrainians in Manitoba and the pivotal role played by Winnipeg — long the spiritual, organizational, and intellectual centre of the Ukrainian-Canadian community — permitted Yuzyk to make the claim that "the progress made by the Ukrainians in Manitoba, as well as their general attitudes and sentiments, may therefore be considered typical of the 400,000 Canadian citizens of Ukrainian extraction."[26]

Following the precedent set by most other students of Ukrainian-Canadian development, Yuzyk began his discussion with a résumé of Ukrainian history that was openly sympathetic to the plight of Ukraine in the twentieth century.[27] He then devoted chapters to Ukrainian immigration and settlement;

progress in agriculture, industry, business, and the professions; religious life; organizations; the press; literature; education and recreation; a Ukrainian-Canadian cultural pattern; participation in public affairs; attitudes during the two world wars; Winnipeg as the Ukrainian-Canadian capital; and the whole process of Canadianization. Although it concentrated on the Manitoba situation to the exclusion of specific developments elsewhere, Yuzyk's study did approach a universal history of Ukrainians in Canada in that it took Manitoba to be the heartland of Ukrainian-Canadian life. One of the shortcomings of the work was that its topical presentation resulted in considerable repetition from chapter to chapter.

By now it should be evident that it was common practice for historians to approach Ukrainian-Canadian immigration and development in a manner similar to the one adopted by Yuzyk, and to measure the rate and the extent of integration within economic, social and political categories. As the body of research grew and as certain facts were established, the material in subsequent histories became more uniform in character. From his discussion of economic progress, vertical mobility, and the inroads being made into new territory, Yuzyk concluded that the Ukrainian-Canadian community — initially characterized by peasant agriculturists and unskilled labourers without an educated leadership — had gradually stratified into classes. The formation of a middle class representing all walks of life had stabilized the community and indicated the progress made by the group.

Another characteristic feature of Ukrainian-Canadian historiography has been a tendency for the author to compromise his objectivity by writing from a point of view that reflected the ideology of a particular group. In Yuzyk's case, an unwarranted anti-communist bias undermined the scholarly tone of his otherwise credible study. The fact that he wrote during the height of the Cold War probably accounted for his insistence that the Communist Party maintained little support among Ukrainian Canadians. Yuzyk argued that most Canadians believed that Ukrainian Canadians were allied with the communist movement and that even their churches were "secretly sympathetic" to the Soviet Union. He protested: "A small but active and vociferous minority directed by Moscow-trained leaders, has created a mirage, which has been increased to such proportions that the public has been led to believe in a Ukrainian-communist bogy."[28]   77

In his detailed discussion of the growth of Ukrainian-Canadian communism, Yuzyk warned that its subversive political goals — the destruction of capitalism in Canada and its replacement by a soviet government — were camouflaged under social and cultural activities:

> . . . the strength of this communist element should not be underestimated. Its activities are supported by a larger number of sympathizers and fellow travellers than are recorded in the membership. The members form a large wing of the communist movement in Canada, which is led by men well trained in revolutionary methods and in propaganda. It is wise to remember that the Bolsheviks in Russia formed no greater proportion when they seized the government in 1917. Fortunately, the large majority of patriotic Ukrainian Canadians are highly conscious of the possible threat of the fifth column in their midst and will not allow the situation to run out of control. Vigilance is the price of the preservation of our democratic institutions.[29]

Clearly, there was nothing covert about Yuzyk's personal politics.

Although Yuzyk's manuscript was essentially complete by 1949, he later appended a summary paragraph to each chapter in which he evaluated developments to 1952, outlined the current situation, and offered some predictions about future trends. His addenda are both interesting and valuable in that they reflected contemporary opinion on the immediate impact and potential influence of the post-World War II Ukrainian immigrants on the established Ukrainian-Canadian community. In many instances the recent immigrants had created their own groups outside of the extant community structures, and this was a growing source of concern among old Ukrainian-Canadians. Yuzyk, however, recognized that the newcomers would give impetus to dying institutions and help to revive Ukrainian traditions, to some extent countering the growing lack of involvement in Ukrainian affairs by Ukrainian-Canadian youth. The Ukrainian-Canadian press, for example, faced a bleak future prior to World War II; yet, it expanded in the post-war years at the same time that its influence continued to wane. A similar pattern was discernible in the activities around community halls, where a decline in participation by increasingly estranged Ukrainian youth was partially reversed with the arrival of displaced persons. Despite the renewed interest and vitality generated by the latest wave of immigrants — among them poets and writers who would contribute much to the quantity and quality of Ukrainian-language literature — the general picture, as drawn by Yuzyk, was one of decline.

Yuzyk's final chapter, "The Process of Canadianization," dealt with the adaptation of Ukrainians to Canadian life. His own preference for the "mosaic" concept of an evolving Canadian identity that retained cultural heritages without political loyalties, became more pronounced in later years, when, as a Canadian senator, he achieved recognition as a spokesman for multiculturalism in Canada.[30] His conclusion to the *The Ukrainians in Manitoba* illustrates this development in his thinking:

> The interplay of economic forces, of democratic practice, of the many cultural traits is slowly welding all its component ethnic groups into one dynamic Canadian nation. As yet, there is no distinctly Canadian culture, but it is in process of formation. Patterns of Canadian behaviour are already becoming evident and from these will come cultural traditions.
>
> In this Canadian mosaic of peoples, the Ukrainian Canadians are consciously or unconsciously making their contribution to the creation of a common Canadian culture. Some Canadian leaders like to think of Canada as a symphony orchestra composed of a variety of instruments which play different notes, but all of which blend to give to the listener a masterpiece of harmonious and inspiring music. Other leaders like to compare Canadian culture to a flower garden in which are beautiful flowers of many varieties, colours, and scents. Among these the Ukrainian flower has its opportunity to blossom forth in rich and exciting beauty. Certain it is, that out of the best elements of the diverse cultures in Canada there will be moulded a superior civilization. To that then the wise leadership of men of understanding, sympathy, and vision, which has been forthcoming constantly from the peoples of Anglo-Saxon stock, may be worthily devoted.[31]

Yuzyk focused on the organized and visible Ukrainian-Canadian community and approached it according to themes, periods, and categories that were largely utilized by subsequent writers on Ukrainian-Canadian history. As it would therefore be redundant   79 to examine much of the most recent work from the standpoint of form and general content, we will restrict our discussion to an assessment of each author's bias, emphasis, and area of concentration.

Fiction and Memoirs

That English-language novelists have neglected the multi-faceted experience of Slavic immigrants in Canada is regrettable in the light of the rich possibilities inherent in the subject matter and the unique challenges posed for any author attempting an artistic understanding of Ukrainian-Canadian development. With the exception of Connor's *The Foreigner,* non-Ukrainian writers have treated Ukrainian Canadians only marginally in their works of fiction.[32] Although much has been written in the Ukrainian language depicting Ukrainian life in Canada,[33] only two novels worthy of attention have to date appeared in English. Since both vividly portrayed life in western Canadian-Ukrainian communities, they may be reviewed in our discussion of Ukrainian-Canadian historiography. The less significant of the two, *Yellow Boots* by Vera Lysenko, was published in 1954. The more substantial work, *Sons of the Soil* by Illia Kiriak — an epic trilogy about a group of Ukrainian immigrant families settling in rural Alberta at the turn of the century — was originally written and published in Ukrainian, but was translated by Michael Luchkovich and published in an abridged version of one volume in 1959.

Yellow Boots was essentially a fictional treatment of a recurring theme in English-language literature on Ukrainian Canadians — assimilation versus the "mosaic." Its central motif concerned the difficult transition from Ukrainian peasant culture to Canadian life in a North American environment, with the author taking the position that while it was necessary to discard what was detrimental and anachronistic in the traditional lifestyle, there was also much of value that deserved recognition.

Lysenko gave a detailed description of life in the Ukrainian village of Prairie Dawn, Manitoba, and the surrounding countryside where the protagonist of the novel, Lilli Landash, grew up. She portrayed the harsh existence of a people whose arduous toil was relieved by religious faith and festivals, and made more bearable by their innate musicality and spontaneous release of emotions through song. The ancient roots of the ritual

cycle of life in this Ukrainian village on the Canadian prairies
were revealed in the folklore, customs, superstitions, and religious
observances of the people. *Yellow Boots* preserved an excellent
record of Ukrainian peasant traditions and lifestyles as they were
practiced for many years in the new homeland.

The quest for material wealth was seen as a threat to the ancient
values — should Ukrainian Canadians lose them, they would
have to live in a spiritual vacuum. Anton Landash — an
unsatisfactory character from the literary standpoint as he was
riddled with too many contradictions[34] — typified the Ukrainian
immigrant settler who enslaved himself and his family to the land
in the bid for economic betterment. Unlike her father, however,
Lilli Landash did not sacrifice herself or the beauty and wisdom
of her heritage in the process of succeeding in Canada. A sensitive
girl who was shunned and abused by her family, she found inner
contentment in the timeless traditions of her people and in the
rhythms, colours, sounds, and motions of the natural world,
which she interpreted in song. Drawing on the resources of her
rich heritage, she discovered the key to successfully adapting her
Ukrainian cultural legacy to life in Canada.

A natural singer responsive to the rhythms around her and
imbued with a sense of the tragic past of Ukraine, Lilli could ease
the trauma of dislocation and soothe the mental anguish of the
immigrants by expressing both their joy and sorrow in her songs.
It was this gift, recognized by her school teacher, Ian MacTavish,
that enabled Lilli to become the interpreter of her people to old
and new Canadians.

With MacTavish's help Lilli migrated to the city, where she
gradually became attuned to an industrial environment; her
discovery and incorporation of the "factory rhythm" marked the
success of her transition to a new life. She joined a workers' folk
choir organized by an Austrian named Matthew Reiner, who
helped fellow immigrants to retain their spiritual roots in the
belief that songs sprang from the people. He reflected on Lilli's
personal transition from the world of nature to the world of
machines:

Was this how the true folk artist translated work rhythms,
whether on the land or in the factory? "She has made the
transition," thought Matthew, "and without losing her natural
touch." The peasants who were forced off the land into
European factories, the peasant immigrants who had gone into   81

American industry, leaving their peasant background behind them — all had been faced with disorientation — the inner rhythm had been lost, naturally enough, reflected Matthew. He had seen the effects, not always happy, in the lives of his own choir members.[35]

In going from a Ukrainian peasant culture to an urban and industrialized Canadian society, Lilli retained those spiritual and cultural strengths from her background which enabled her to accommodate herself to the new world.

The "yellow boots" in the novel — of sentimental value to Lilli's mother as she had been wearing them when she first met her husband and now associated them with the Carpathian homeland of her youth — became a symbol of the old world and its dwindling legacy. Significantly, the boots had been worn by Lilli's eldest sister at her wedding, but they were shunned by the younger sisters who saw them as relics of the past and favoured Canadian customs and styles. Lilli's rebellion against her father when he tried to force her to marry the vulgar Zachary for selfish reasons, drove her to MacTavish for guidance and prompted the following observation:

> Why was it at this moment MacTavish suddenly thought of two opposite images — the image of Anton's great tan peasant boots as MacTavish had seen them tramping across the furrows of his newly-broken earth, and the contrasting image of the dancing yellow boots of Fialka as he had seen them at that wedding — how long ago — three years? The ruthless strides of the pioneer, beating out their harsh rhythms, crushing anything delicate that might come into their path, and the exuberant rhythm of dancing boots, tracing a pattern of joyous color: these two pictures symbolized for MacTavish the beauty and brutality in the heritage of these people. Was it not asking too much of these unlearned immigrants, he thought, that they should pause in the midst of their pioneering labours to decide how much of that beauty they should retain, how much surrender of their brutality.[36]

Later, while on a singing tour in rural Manitoba, Lilli was drawn to the family farm, where she noticed the improvements that mechanization and modernization had brought. Her father was now an old man, "diminished by all he had given" to the land; her brother Peter was a student at an agricultural college. Her mother wore a city dress and had her hair done in a permanent wave, neither of which suited her as had a peasant blouse and braids. But mother and daughter found common ground in their preference for the old and their dislike of soulless machinery. The yellow boots rightfully became Lilli's. As she sang to her family and neighbours, she reflected: "It was strange . . . that she who had fled that environment had built her life upon all the old traditions which had constituted its essence, while those who had remained behind had yielded to modernism."[37] On asking her brother what she could do for her people, he replied:

> Take back with you what is best in our past and preserve it for us . . . The land, that is our job . . . but yours is to cherish the old and give it new meaning. Through these songs, other people in our country can look into the hearts of our people, whom they once despised, and see what beauty is there. You'll speak for all of us.[38]

Yellow Boots is not a memorable contribution to literature — its characterization is somewhat shallow and unnatural, and the plot itself is uncohesive — but it is valuable as a record of Ukrainian peasant customs and beliefs as they were practiced by first generation Ukrainians in Canada. It is also a useful document depicting the material and spiritual adaptation of Ukrainians to Canadian life, showing the way certain traditional values and skills could be preserved in the urban and industrial environment of the twentieth century. Lilli's success in synthesizing with her songs, the old world and the new, was an example to all immigrants, for besides sharing the treasures of her culture with fellow Canadians, she also enriched the lives of her own people.

Illia Kiriak's *Sons of the Soil* was a much more realistic attempt at depicting Ukrainian-Canadian life than was *Yellow Boots,* though it dealt only indirectly with the issues of assimilation and acculturation. It is an excellent fictional account of the experiences of five Ukrainian families — the Workuns, the Poshtars, the Dubs, the Wakars, and the Solowys—homesteading in Alberta. The work chronicles the initial hardships, physical suffering, and primitive existence of the pioneers; their homesickness, their neighbourliness, and their wonder at the bounty of Canada; the necessity for men and young women to 83 seek wage-labour employment away from their families to accumulate the money to buy livestock and farm implements; and, finally, the progress made by the community, marked by the first threshing and the replacement of oxen with horse power. The story explores the deep-seated desire of the settlers for traditional religion — their need for spiritual nourishment and ritual celebration to cope with the monotony and hardship of grinding toil — and it records their joy at the arrival of the first priest. It also covers the organization and operation of a school district, and the pioneers' gradual introduction to Canadian democracy and laws.

Kiriak's characters are representative of the different types of personalities who settled Canada, interacted, and gradually evolved into an identifiable community. Workun is presented as the model pioneer and the natural leader of the group; Dub represents the doubt-ridden immigrant who pays the price of disillusionment for his vacillations. Poshtar, the first settler in the region and hence the mediator between the group and the outside world, becomes the government presence in the colony — postmaster, and secretary-treasurer of the newly-created school district — besides reaping the rewards of being storekeeper and creditor for the entire community. In his role as interpreter and go-between he informs a priest who is reluctant to be involved in a mixed marriage, that in Canada it was money, and not faith, that measured the value of a man.

In time, the immigrants developed physical and spiritual roots in the virgin soil of western Canada. The death of a child named Semen, during the first summer on the homestead, gave the immigrants their first claim to the new land:

> Thus it came about that little Semen found a grave in the virgin plain, a resting place marked by a large cross set firmly in alien soil, no longer alien by reason of his death. And the ancient symbol, which was like a challenge to the empty land seemed to say that this child and those of his blood were now dedicated to the task of transforming the wilderness into a Christian civilization.[39]

The ambivalent memories of the first year in Canada — the cold winter they survived in draughty houses and inadequate clothing, as well as the joyous singing of carols at Christmas — remained vividly in the minds of the settlers in their later years.

Sons of the Soil ends as it began with the reminiscences of the last surviving settler of the original group — Hrehory Workun. When he dies it is the son of another pioneer, Toma Wakar, now a graduate in agriculture, who offers this eulogy to those first Ukrainian settlers:

Their physical remains are buried here; but their good deeds will be treasured forever in the memories of succeeding generations. For they were genuine *Sons of the Soil* who blazed a trail that we who came after might find a less onerous and fuller life.[40]

As a classic portrayal of Ukrainian immigrant life, *Sons of the Soil* has yet to be equalled.

Although Ukrainian Canadians have been prolific in the writing of Ukrainian-language autobiographies, there has been little parallel activity in English. This is unfortunate as the Ukrainian-language memoirs of teachers, homesteaders, and community leaders contain a wealth of information on the early years of Ukrainian life in Canada from personal perspectives. Of three English-language Ukrainian-Canadian autobiographies, only one merits recognition as a permanent contribution to Ukrainian-Canadian historiography. It is *A Ukrainian Canadian in Parliament: Memoirs of Michael Luchkovich,* the auto-biography of the first Ukrainian-Canadian Member of Parliament. Of less significance have been *Taking Root in Canada: An Autobiography* by Gus Romaniuk, and *My Heritage from the Builders of Canada* by Olivia Rose Fry.

Taking Root in Canada, an English translation of a Ukrainian manuscript, was published in 1954.[41] It recounted the life story of Gus Romaniuk, who, in 1912 as a boy of eleven, had immigrated to his father's homestead at Riverton, Manitoba. As the elder Romaniuk was among the immigrants who farmed the forbidding marshlands of the Interlake Region of Manitoba, the securing of outside employment and supplementary sources of income was a necessity. Romaniuk himself was successively a logger, farmhand, construction worker, railway labourer, fisherman, barber, merchant, cattlemen, fur trader, and eventually hotelman and councillor in Riverton. His checkered career, extending from Saskatchewan to Ontario, was illustrative of the practice of Ukrainian immigrants to obtain wage-labour employment to subsidize or escape their farming operations.

85

Romaniuk resided in a predominantly Icelandic community where Ukrainians appeared to be a relatively passive minority. There is no indication that the author participated in Ukrainian activities beyond his youth or that an organized Ukrainian community existed in the vicinity. Although he remained conscious of his origins, Romaniuk emphasized social and economic intercourse regardless of nationality. With the exception of two chapters — the first and the last — which specifically concerned the Ukrainian immigrant experience, Romaniuk's autobiography could just as easily have been written by any number of non-Ukrainian pioneers. Consequently, *Taking Root in Canada* is of limited value to Ukrainian-Canadian historiography outside of its depiction of economic adaptation and experimentation when farming failed.

Olivia Fry's autobiography, *My Heritage from the Builders of Canada,* was published in 1967, and is interesting as an account of the author's development from her youthful desire to escape her ethnic background to her later regret and shame for not having given her children an appreciation of their Ukrainian heritage. Fry's childhood recollections of homestead life in Alberta and incidents from her adult years are placed against the background of her pilgrimage to Ukraine and the Bukovinian village of her parents. Her stories of the hardships encountered by her parents vividly exemplify the struggles of the Ukrainian settler to "found his kingdom" in the new world.

That Fry openly admired the Soviet regime was made clear by the fact that she included without comment the Great Russian interpretation of Ukrainian history as told her by a cousin at the University of Chernivtsi.[42] Particularly interesting was her observation of a difference in attitude between Galicians and Bukovinians regarding the nature of Soviet rule. Commenting on Galician rebelliousness and resistance and Bukovinian acquiescence, she reproachfully related how a communal farm at Lviv had deliberately cultivated weeds to spite the inspector and Communist Party functionaries. Her own sympathies obviously lay with the Bukovinians: "We felt fortunate that we went to Chernovtsi [Bukovina] because had we visited Lvov [Galicia] only we would have had a different opinion of Russia altogether."[43] Outside of its description of Ukrainian pioneer life in Alberta and its documentation of the evolution of a second-generation Ukrainian Canadian from initial rejection to the rediscovery of native pride, *My Heritage from the Builders of*

Canada has little merit. Not only is it ungrammatical and incorrectly punctuated, but unfolds in a confused and haphazard fashion and is written in the most elementary of styles.

Published in 1965, *A Ukrainian Canadian in Parliament: Memoirs of Michael Luchkovich* is the record of the life and thoughts of a man who was once an important symbol of Ukrainian-Canadian development and integration on a national scale. Luchkovich, born in Pennsylvannia to Ukrainian immigrants, came to Canada in 1907 to attend Manitoba College. It was here that his objective Ukrainianness evolved into a conscious cultivation of the Ukrainian language and ethnic associations. In 1912 he came to Alberta where he taught in various rural Ukrainian schools until his election to federal parliament in 1926 as the United Farmers of Alberta representative of the predominantly Ukrainian constituency of Vegreville. He held his seat until 1935, when defeat sent him plummeting into years of mental depression and ill health. He operated a small grocery store in Edmonton until his declining health forced him to abandon it in 1959. In his later years Luchkovich translated several Ukrainian-language works into English.

A Ukrainian Canadian in Parliament is a personal account of Luchkovich's activities, contributions, thoughts, and observations as the first Ukrainian Canadian to be elected to the House of Commons. He cites his vocal opposition to Polish pacification attempts in Western Ukraine in the inter-war years and his defence of Ukrainian Canadians against the denunciations of Bishop George Exton Lloyd, as two of the highlights of his parliamentary career.[44] As a Canadian delegate to the International Inter-Parliamentary Union Congress staged in Romania in 1931, Luchkovich laments the inability of the League of Nations to intervene in the Ukrainian situation.

Luchkovich's autobiography explores his philosophy of life, and, with remarkable candour often conveys the impression that he was a man groping for something spiritual to give him a sense of inner peace and direction. Extolling the virtues of freedom and democracy, Luchkovich defends the dual nature of his loyalty with the assertion that "loyalty to the Ukrainians does not mean disloyalty to the country of my adoption."[45] Despite his introspective analysis of his beliefs, Luchkovich fails to clarify the details of his personal development, especially the factors behind his growing involvement with the Ukrainian-Canadian community, why he became interested in Ukrainian problems, and

87

how his concern for the farming population propelled him into the camp of the United Farmers of Alberta. Was his candidacy based primarily on ethnic or ideological grounds? He confesses that it was the desire to be famous which led him into politics and writing but Luchkovich fails to mention when and under what circumstances he became a Canadian citizen. It is unfortunate that in an autobiography where the author frequently submits to self-analysis, more attention could not have been paid to intellectual development. Since Luchkovich was the first Ukrainian Canadian to ascend to national prominence and become a spokesman for his people, one regrets the omissions in his reminiscences.

With a number of excellent fictional and autobiographical accounts available in the Ukrainian language, it is to be hoped that similar publications in English will increase, either as translations are made or new works are written. Memoirs in particular are wealthy storehouses of information on Ukrainian-Canadian life. To date, the language barrier has made most autobiographies inaccessible to those who are outside the linguistic group.

Bilingualism and Biculturalism and the Canadian Centennial

In 1963 the federal government established the Laurandeau-Dunton[46] Royal Commission on Bilingualism and Biculturalism in Canada. Its activities were to dominate the period of national reassessment that accompanied the celebration of Canada's centennial. The question of Canadian identity was posed in terms of either a bilingual and bicultural character based on the two founding races, or a multilingual and multicultural composite that recognized the equal partnership of all of the ethnic groups within the country. Ukrainian presentations at the hearings of the Commission were exceeded in number only by those of English and French Canadians. Book IV of the Commission's report was published in 1970 under the title *Cultural Contribution of the Other Ethnic Groups,* and it reflected the influence of a well-organized and vocal Ukrainian-Canadian community. The leading role played by Ukrainian Canadians in the campaign to win official recognition of multiculturalism and multilingualism left them open to the criticism of some of their fellow Canadians. Advocates of the policy, however, took the task with a sense of mission, confident that they were making a great contribution to Canada's national development.

In 1966 Elizabeth D. Wangenheim published an article, "The Ukrainians: A Case Study of the 'Third Force'," in *Nationalism in Canada,* a collection of essays edited by Peter Russell. In it she expressed reservations regarding Ukrainian-Canadian demands for special recognition of the Ukrainian language and culture, especially if such a position were adopted as a prototype by other groups in Canada. Wangenheim accurately perceived that Ukrainian-Canadian agitation for multiculturalism, and, more crucially, the continued existence of their group as an identifiable and viable entity lay in the fact that, unlike other ethnic groups in Canada, they lacked an independent motherland and thus deemed it their responsibility to preserve the Ukrainian language and culture in the "diaspora." Hence, as they were "an extreme example of the effects which 'nationalism without autonomy' can have upon the integration of immigrants into a society such as Canada's,"[47] Ukrainians were a special case complicating the quest for a Canadian identity.

Wangenheim examined the peculiar position of Ukrainian Canadians in terms of the history of Ukrainian nationalism in Europe; Ukrainian immigration and settlement in Canada as it absorbed, reacted to, and reflected the nationalist movement in Ukraine; and the impact of Ukrainian nationalism within the Canadian "mosaic." From their beginnings in Canada Ukrainians had been conspicuously defensive of their language and culture but the unity they had achieved during World War II with the triumph of more moderate elements oriented towards Canadian goals, was challenged and undermined by the arrival of European-oriented political refugees after 1945:

By constantly claiming that the USSR's Russification tactics pose a threat to the continued existence of a Ukrainian language and culture, they have created within many of the younger generation, born or educated here, a sense of commitment — an obligation to fight for the perpetuation of the Ukrainian language, the glorification of Ukrainian history and culture, its myths and symbols. This appeal tends to be more powerful than all the pressures working towards a dissolution of close in-groups ties — both the pressures of intergenerational cross-cultural conflict and the monetary and social attractions of the larger society. While this appeal probably has the greatest impact on post-war immigrants and their children, it also finds a response among many of the

89

Canadian-born Ukrainians who have been baffled in their attempts to be 'just Canadian' by their failure to perceive any solid content in Canadian identity. . . . Thus, the post-war immigration which aided in raising the image of 'the immigrant' in the eyes of the host society also created a counter-structure diminishing the likelihood of the early cultural and structural assimilation of minority ethnic groups into a more homogeneous society.[48]

As each ethnic group in Canada appeared to be interested solely in its own heritage and discouraged outsiders from participating in its activities, Wangenheim questioned the validity of the very concept "mosaic." At the same time that Ukrainians — along with other ethnic groups — resented adopting Canadian symbols of British and French origin, they failed to justify the relevance of Shevchenko, Ukrainian literature, and Cossack tales to non-Ukrainian Canadians. Although some ethnic groups were satisfied, maintaining their language and culture through their own financial resources and efforts, Ukrainians were not. Wangenheim saw that such demands as the teaching of Ukrainian in public schools, Ukrainian programs on the CBC, and the consideration of Ukrainian-language literature for the Governor-General's Award, meant the expenditure of public funds to promote the interests of a specific group. Granting Ukrainian Canadians special status could initiate a trend.

National oppression, cultural genocide in the form of Russification, and the struggle to obtain recognition as a nationality impelled émigré Ukrainians to preserve the Ukrainian language and culture abroad and to project their image of Ukrainian identity without considering the implications of such strident identification on Canadian unity. Expressing the fear that acceptance of Ukrainian Canadians as spokesmen for the "Third Force" could endanger Canadian unity, Wangenheim concluded:

. . . regardless of the diversity which may exist among minority ethnic groups, the concept of the Third Force is acquiring wide currency in Canadian political thought and there is an equally wide tendency to perceive the Ukrainians as the spokesmen of this force. If, as a result of these developments, other minority groups should come to regard the Ukrainians as a model of what an ethnic group's position *should* be, then many of them, regardless of their own different history and relationship to their homeland, might come to expect the same type of treatment as the Ukrainians. In this event, the difficulties involved in coping with the basic problem of Canadian identity might well be intensified.[49]

Curiously, Wangenheim did not state whether or not she considered the Ukrainian position justified in the light of Ukrainian historical experience and the predicament of contemporary Ukraine: that she felt it potentially detrimental to Canadian interests is clear. Her thesis is a significant commentary on the response of the Ukrainian-Canadian community to the bilingualism and biculturalism debate. It is of particular interest when considered in the context of other studies of Ukrainian-Canadian history published in conjunction with the Canadian Centennial.

In 1964 Vladimir J. Kaye published his major contribution to Ukrainian-Canadian historiography, *Early Ukrainian Settlements in Canada 1895-1900: Dr. Josef Oleskow's Role in the Settlement of the Canadian Northwest.* The first in a series of cultural, historical, and sociological research projects sponsored by the Ukrainian Canadian Research Foundation,[50] Kaye's account of the earliest Ukrainian immigration to Canada — from an official perspective — has been an invaluable addition to both Ukrainian and Canadian history. He made extensive use of primary and documentary source material, particularly government files and papers, to provide a well-researched and thoroughly documented, factual, and chronological record of developments. Although the book contained little in the way of interpretation and showed only minimal concern about the human element involved, it fulfilled the author's objective and is rich in useful source material. [Author's note: Kaye used the Polish spelling "Oleskow" throughout his book, but I prefer the Ukrainian spelling "Oleskiw," which will be used here.]

The first part of *Early Ukrainian Settlements in Canada* dealt with Oleskiw's role in initiating the Ukrainian exodus to Canada, his Canadian tour of 1895, his selective immigration scheme for an orderly movement of farmers with means to be assisted by the Canadian government, and his attempts to regulate Ukrainian immigration on both sides of the Atlantic in the years from 1895 to 1900. Kaye examined the correspondence between Oleskiw and various Canadian government officials, intergovernmental communiques, and Oleskiw's two pamphlets — *Pro vil'ni zemli* and *O emigratsii*[51] — to provide a comprehensive chronicle of events. He considered the support Oleskiw received from the *Prosvita* ("Enlightenment") Society in Lviv in promoting Ukrainian immigration to Canada over Brazil, the reaction of the Ukrainian intellectual community in Galicia to Oleskiw's proposals, and the efforts of Ukrainian popular educational societies to facilitate the movement. Kaye also discussed the opposition of the Austrian government and the Polish faction in the Vienna Parliament to a mass movement of peasant agriculturalists. He thus explored the socio-political background to the mass migration instead of simplifying it to a Canadian recruitment of agricultural settlers coinciding with Galician aspirations to escape economic destitution and political oppression. Viewed as an Austro-Galician phenomenon initiated in Galicia by concerned Ukrainians on official and semi-official levels, Kaye's original research shed new light on the nature of Ukrainian immigration to Canada. Previous histories had not approached the subject from a European angle.

Kaye's findings established the fact that the groundwork for the admission of the "men in sheepskin coats" had been laid prior to the administration of Clifford Sifton; it was his immediate predecessors in the Department of the Interior who had initially responded to the advances and enquiries of Oleskiw. Kaye contended that if the Canadian government had recognized the wisdom in Oleskiw's scheme for supervised and assisted immigration, many of the ensuing difficulties and hardships encountered by both government officials and the immigrants themselves, could have been avoided.[52] Transferred at the turn of the century from his position as Professor of Agriculture at the Teachers' Seminary in Lviv to the Directorship of the Teachers' Seminary at Sokal, Oleskiw's activities in Ukrainian immigration dwindled and finally ceased. His health gradually deteriorated, and he died in 1903. Today, although largely forgotten, Oleskiw "nevertheless deserves at least a modest niche among the builders of the Canadian West for having initiated and for five years vigorously and successfully propagated the emigration of Ukrainian settlers to Canada."[53]

Part Two of *Early Ukrainian Settlements in Canada* probed the founding and development (to approximately 1900) of the first Ukrainian colonies in Canada: Stuartburn, Dauphin, Pleasant Home, Strathclair, and Shoal Lake in Manitoba;

Rosthern and Yorkton in Saskatchewan; and Edna-Star in
Alberta, the oldest Ukrainian settlement in Canada. Utilizing
government reports, intergovernmental correspondence, and
communiques, as well as Ukrainian memoirs and travelogues,
Kaye was able to depict, factually and statistically, the fortunes of
these communities during their formative years. One comes to
appreciate the magnitude of the task facing Canadian government officials in settling and managing so many people who
spoke an unfamiliar tongue and had alien customs and habits.
The documents recorded the conflicts that often resulted when
government officials tried to control the placing of each colonist
in opposition to the adamant desire of many immigrants to settle
near friends and relatives. They also conveyed the impression that
the civil servants responsible were sincerely concerned with the
fate of the Ukrainian immigrants in their charge.[54] In addition,
Kaye dispelled the myth that the first wave of Ukrainian immigrants to Canada consisted solely of poverty-stricken peasants.
Many were peasants of means while others came from the long-
impoverished Ukrainian nobility. Kaye noted in a summary
chapter the situation by 1900, the increasing prosperity of these
colonies, their physical expansion, integration, and growing
interest in municipal affairs, schools, and churches. He
concluded:

> Dr. Oleskow never doubted that the Ukrainian settlers and
> their children would "become very soon truly Canadians," as
> he wrote in one of his letters to the Minister of the Interior in
> 1896. Oleskow's unstinting efforts on behalf of his people and
> his tireless striving to improve their lot through emigration to
> Canada have indeed been well rewarded — his vision has come
> true.[55]

A final section in *Early Ukrainian Settlements in Canada*
contained biographical sketches of Ukrainian, Canadian, and
Austrian figures important to the early years of Ukrainian
immigration to Canada. Kaye also provided indices of surnames
and place names.

Through his analysis of the material at his disposal, Kaye was
able to correct certain misconceptions and distortions regarding
the composition of the Ukrainian immigrants, the impetus behind
their movement, and the details of their settlement. His
recognition of Oleskiw's contribution to the policies that shaped   93

the immigration of Ukrainians to Canada has added a new dimension to our understanding of the history of the opening of the Canadian West. *Early Ukrainian Settlements in Canada* is a reliable account of the specifics behind the inauguration of Ukrainian immigration to Canada, and as such is essential reading for anyone interested in Ukrainian-Canadian pioneering history.

In 1965 the First National Conference on Canadian Slavs was held at Banff, Alberta, followed by a second conference in Ottawa in 1968. The proceedings of both sessions were published in two volumes entitled *Slavs in Canada*.[56] They contained numerous articles on various aspects of Ukrainian-Canadian life. Charles W. Hobart presented the results of a sociological survey in a paper on the "Adjustment of Ukrainians in Alberta: Alienation and Integration." "Some Demographic Aspects of the Ukrainian Population in Canada," by Warren E. Kalbach, investigated the degree to which the demographic character of Ukrainians in Canada approached or diverged from general Canadian patterns. V.J. Kaye, in "Three Phases of Ukrainian Immigration," provided an excellent summary of the characteristics and outlooks of each wave of Ukrainian immigration to Canada, and Elizabeth D. Wangenheim's presentation at the Banff Conference — entitled "Problems of Research on Ukrainians in Eastern Canada" — set forth the obstacles that she encountered when researching the Ukrainians of Metropolitan Toronto as a sociologist and a non-Slav.

At the Ottawa conference, M. Chomiak spoke on "Contributions of Ukrainians to the Development and Growth of Schools in Alberta," concluding that the Ukrainian share in the development of Alberta's school system was greater than the Ukrainian proportion of the population of that province. W. Janishewskyj, in "Ukrainian Engineers in Ontario," utilized sample case histories to illustrate the Ukrainian contribution to engineering since World War II. Similarly, V.J. Kaye presented a paper on "Early Ukrainian Graduates of Agricultural Colleges," furnishing pertinent personal data for forty-six such graduates between 1921 and 1941 and describing their subsequent agricultural achievements as individuals and researchers working for federal and provincial institutions. A. Maslanyk and M. Chomiak discussed the accomplishments of various scientists of Ukrainian background in "The Scientific Contribution of

Ukrainians to the Industrial Development of Canada," while M.

Plawiuk briefly examined Ukrainian Credit Unions in Canada. In "Studies in Ukrainian Literature in Canada," Orest Pawliw identified dominant literary trends such as the tendency of authors to examine problems and themes that were either banned or distorted in the literature of Soviet Ukraine. "Ukrainian Free Academy of Science — UVAN of Canada," by Jaroslav B. Rudnyckyj, examined yet another facet of intellectual activity and organization in the Ukrainian-Canadian community, while John H. Syrnick, in "The Ukrainian Canadian Committee: Its Significance in the Canadian Society," sketched the formation of that body, its principles, objectives, and achievements.

A particularly interesting paper, "The Development of Political Socialization of the Ukrainians in Alberta," was presented to the Ottawa Conference by Sidney I. Pobihushchy. The political socialization (i.e., the induction of an individual or group into the political life of a community or society) of four groups of Alberta Ukrainians — three based on the successive waves of immigration, the fourth being comprised of the Canadian-born or Canadian-raised children of immigrants — was examined in terms of the hypothesis that a strong relationship existed between the nature and degree of immigrant politicization and the original political environment that spawned and shaped them. Pobihushchy concluded that the first two immigrant groups, from parochial and imperial political backgrounds respectively, were oriented first to local and only secondarily to federal politics. Their socialization into Canadian politics was gradual except for the traumatic experience of the Depression, when the most common sentiment expressed by those of the second immigration was a growing disenchantment with Canadian life feeding a desire to return to their native land. The third immigration, highly politicized and nationalistic in outlook because of its participation in political parties and independence movements in Europe, gravitated primarily to federal politics, seeing participation in the national political arena as the key to the safeguarding of their Ukrainian identity. Canadian-born Ukrainians generally followed Canadian patterns of political socialization.

A final paper presented at the Ottawa Conference was "Ukrainian Church Architecture in Canada," read by Radoslav Zuk. He characterized three phases of Ukrainian church architecture in Canada: the early vernacular phase introduced by the original immigrants, the disorientation phase characterized by an absence of plan or design or by the revival of a pseudo-baroque style, and a recent attempt by a small number of architects to synthesize traditional architectural forms with those found in the contemporary environment of urban Canada.

In sum, *Slavs in Canada* covered a spectrum of topics and quality of research on Ukrainian Canadians. Full of useful and interesting information, they are an indication of the diversifying approaches being taken to Ukrainian-Canadian history.

As the seventy-fifth anniversary of Ukrainian settlement in Canada in 1966 almost coincided with the celebration of the Canadian Centennial a year later, numerous commemorative histories were published. Appearing at the height of the debate on bilingualism and biculturalism — characterized by the growing popularity of the concept of multiculturalism — the studies reflected Ukrainian-Canadian concern for the official protection of their language and culture and its entrenchment into Canadian life. In general, these works argued for both the integration and the perpetuation of a distinctly Ukrainian-Canadian culture and identity within Canadian society.

The first publication to commemorate these landmark years was *Tribute to our Ukrainian Pioneers in Canada's First Century,* a record of the proceedings of a special convention, held in 1966 by the Association of United Ukrainian Canadians (AUUC) and the Workers' Benevolent Association (WBA), to mark the seventy-fifth anniversary of Ukrainian settlement in Canada. Sponsored as it was by two leftist organizations, the conference revealed an obvious communist and pro-Soviet bias in its program. It even received congratulatory messages from Ukraine, including a special broadcast by Radio Kiev from the kinsmen of the first Ukrainian immigrants from Nebyliw.[57] Greetings from the Soviet Ambassador to Canada were conveyed by the First Secretary of the embassy, who dismissed as propaganda the charges that linguistic and cultural genocide were part of the policy of Soviet Ukraine and instead spoke of the fraternity demonstrated by the Joint Convention and its expression of fellowship with 'brother Ukrainians' in the USSR. A superficial, unscholarly and laudatory booklet, *Tribute to our Ukrainian Pioneers in Canada's First Century* nevertheless offers a point of view that stands in sharp contrast to that taken by the majority of Ukrainian-Canadian writers.

The booklet is a compilation of individual speeches given on various aspects of Ukrainian-Canadian life. The dominant themes to emerge dealt with the exploitation and discrimination experienced by the immigrants at the hands of the Anglo-Saxon ruling class. The following passage is fairly typical:

> Historians will one day record that our pioneer immigrants were brought to this country on the lowest possible terms. They were lauded as fine specimens of brawn and muscle, for their prodigious capacity to perform back-breaking work, but were rejected and reviled as specimens of humanity.
> The shocking truth is that the early immigrants from Eastern Europe were the victims of racism in the new land. It was a cross that they bore, together with their first-born, for the greater part of their 75 years here and the bruises of that burden are still painful to the touch.[58]

The immigrants' struggle for human rights was seen to have been initiated by those still-maligned socialist and communist organizations that were the predecessors of the AUUC and WBA, and who had gradually raised the consciousness of Ukrainian Canadians and stirred them to assert their human dignity. It was up to these "progressive" Ukrainian Canadians to "maintain and encourage ties of culture and friendship with the ancestral well-spring of Ukrainian culture — Ukrainian SSR."[59]

In general, *Tribute to our Ukrainian Pioneers in Canada's First Century* is of a very limited value to Ukrainian-Canadian historiography as its repeated emphasis on discrimination and exploitation undermines and overshadows any other useful information. It is interesting, however, as an alternative inter-pretation of the Ukrainian experience in Canada.

In 1967 Wasyl Veryha submitted to the University of Ottawa his M.A. thesis, "The Ukrainian Canadian Committee: Its Origin and War Activity." A factual, step-by-step narrative of the events that led to the creation of that body — including the factional bickering that had to be overcome — and its activities during World War II, Veryha's thesis also embraced the concept of Ukrainian Canadians being part of the "Third Element" in Canada. The "most dynamic and best organized ethnic group" within the "Third Element," Ukrainian Canadians, according to Veryha, had attained this position only with the formation of the Ukrainian Canadian Committee and the burial of internecine disputes. Veryha outlined his objective in the following words:

The present work is an attempt to present the difficulties encountered by the Ukrainian Canadian community in the process of the formation of the Canadian nation and the complexity of the Canadian society at large. Since Canada is celebrating her Centennial year it seems to be a proper time to analyze the place and role of the Ukrainian community in the process of the building of a Canadian nation. The Ukrainian Canadian Committee as a co-ordinating and representative centre, has contributed a great deal to the reduction, if not to the elimination, of the detrimental dissension among Ukrainians, which hurt not only the Ukrainian Canadian community but also the Canadian society in general, especially during the war years.[60]

In the author's opinion, the activities of the Ukrainian Canadian Committee provided an excellent example of how a well-organized and united ethnic group could make a valuable contribution to the building of Canada.

A pamphlet by William Darcovich, *Ukrainians in Canada: The Struggle to Retain their Identity,* published in 1967 under the auspices of the Ottawa Branch of the Ukrainian Self-Reliance Association, explored the oft-alluded to but as yet unexamined problem of the dual identity of Ukrainian Canadians. Of the desire to remain a distinct cultural group while integrating into Canadian society, Darcovich commented:

I became convinced that these efforts were not simply casual and that if the Ukrainians had experienced any success in developing and maintaining an identity in this dual sense it was because of their strong and conscious efforts to do so, often under difficult conditions. To do as much in the future will require even more effort and this struggle for identity is the main theme of this work.[61]

Since further Ukrainian immigration in contemporary circumstances seemed unlikely, Darcovich argued that the future of the Ukrainian-Canadian community would be determined by the character of its present membership and the influences of the social environment of Canada and the United States.

Despite the persistent efforts of Ukrainian Canadians to win acceptance of the "mosaic" concept of Canadian nationhood and thereby confirm their unique position as a people without an independent homeland, several factors were seen to be operating towards the disintegration of such an identity. First, the migration to urban industrial areas, where the majority of the Ukrainian-Canadian population now lives, undermined the continued existence of a distinct community as assimilative forces were stronger in cities than they had been in the homogeneous rural blocs. Secondly, the Ukrainian language continued to be threatened despite the efforts of Ukrainian private schools, the successful introduction of Ukrainian into the public school system and post-secondary institutions, and the statistically higher rate of retention of the mother tongue among Ukrainian Canadians. At the same time, the sharp increase in intermarriage was eroding allegiance to the two traditional churches. With the declining influence of family and church in the face of increasing urbanization and secularization, it was becoming more and more difficult to preserve specifically Ukrainian cultural patterns and values. And the fact that Ukrainian Canadians occupied lower levels on the educational and occupational scales was an indication of their imperfect integration in these spheres. Darcovich concluded:

> While the Ukrainians were able to develop and maintain a separate identity under predominantly rural conditions, it will be more difficult to do the same in the urban environment in which they now live; at the same time the opportunities which city life offers should make it easier for the Ukrainians to reduce the educational and occupational disparities which have become rooted among them. The challenge to the future growth and development of the Ukrainians will be to overcome these important disparities and still continue to maintain a distinct entity.[62]

Like other Ukrainian-Canadian writers reflecting on their community during the centennial year, Darcovich emphasized the duality of the Ukrainian-Canadian identity. However, he did not consider that dual nature to be evidence of an entirely successful or permanent cultural synthesis, noting both the obstacles that continued to bar the way to complete integration into Canadian life, and the threatened existence of the Ukrainian language and culture in twentieth-century urban Canada.

Paul Yuzyk, on the other hand, simply glorified the achievements of the community without acknowledging the

Frances Swyripa

serious problems it faced, in his popular account of Ukrainian-
Canadian history, *Ukrainian Canadians: Their Place and Role in
Canadian Life.* The book was published in 1967 by the Ukrainian
Canadian Professional and Business Federation as its Centennial
project. Not claiming to have written a definitive treatise on the
subject (the book was merely an outline and lacked an overview
and depth), Yuzyk sketched the characteristics of Ukrainian
immigration and settlement; distribution in areas of Canada;
achievements in agriculture, business, industry, the professions,
politics and literature; contributions in government services and
the military forces; cultural and educational progress; church life;
and organizational structure.[63] In an attempt to illustrate how
much Ukrainians have added to the general prosperity and
enrichment of Canadian life — to prove the degree of their
integration and their right to full partnership — Yuzyk listed the
numerous individuals of Ukrainian descent who had achieved
prominence in various fields. Full partnership, Yuzyk argued,
should be extended to all members of the so-called "Third
Element" although Ukrainian Canadians had to date out-
distanced other ethnic groups in such endeavours as participation
in the political life of the nation.

Yuzyk singled out the creation of the Ukrainian Canadian
Committee as the highlight of Ukrainian-Canadian history, and
described its mission in the following words:

> . . . to promote the positive participation of the Ukrainian
> group in Canadian politics, in the cultural evolution of this
> country and in all aspects of its economic and social life, as
> responsible partners with the British, the French, and the other
> ethnic groups of our Canadian nation; emphasis is placed on
> the distinctive cultural identity of the Ukrainian Canadian
> community as a valuable component of the Canadian nation.[64]

The Committee's presentations to the Royal Commission on
Bilingualism and Biculturalism, demanding official recognition
of multiculturalism, made Canadians aware of the vitality of the
Ukrainian-Canadian community and its importance and commitment to Canadian life. "Through the Committee the
Ukrainian Canadians have negotiated with the federal and
provincial governments, with universities and municipal
governments as Canadians and because of their achievements,
united leadership and efforts have won national stature and some
recognition as partners."[65]

It was Yuzyk's opinion that the "Third Element" in general merited greater consideration since it was becoming more articulate in voicing its needs and was demonstrating inter-group co-operation and harmony; hence, it was ready to assume greater responsibilities as a full and equal partner in Confederation. Its demands were all-encompassing:

> Anxious to be a positive force supporting the development of a strong democratic Canadian nation composed of the finest treasures of the various cultures, based on the concept of "unity in continuing diversity" and equality of all citizens, the Third Element ethnic groups want to see more and proper recognition given to them in history books and other school-texts, in CBC programmes, in government bodies such as the Canada Council, Centennial Commission etc., in the Canadian Expo and exhibits of embassies, publications and in appointments on merit to the Senate, cabinet portfolios, judgeships, and offices of Lieutenant-Governors and even of the Governor-General. To promote the full participation of all our citizens in the cultural growth of the Canadian nation, the time has come for the establishment of federal Department of Culture.[66]

Yuzyk was clearly asking for the recognition and development of the "Third Force" as a vital element within Canadian society. In this regard, *Ukrainian Canadians: Their Place and Role in Canadian Life* went beyond its definition as a history of Ukrainians in Canada. It served as an excellent vehicle for Yuzyk's championing of multiculturalism and the "Third Element" as a force in Canadian life.

He concluded with an explanation of the historic "mission" of Ukrainian Canadians and in the process provided them with a raison d'être for their continued existence as an identifiable group within Canadian society. According to Yuzyk, it was the responsibility of Ukrainian Canadians to inform the government and their fellow citizens of the dangers of communism and the necessity of vigilance to prevent its expansion. For this reason they deserved a larger role in the formulation and execution of Canadian foreign policy. In addition, Ukrainians in Canada had played a leading role in promoting ethnic consciousness and, being members of the "Third Element," could serve as a unifying bond between the two founding races.[67] Yuzyk concluded:

101

> If we succeed, and we are well on the road to succeeding, to
> evolve the pattern of unity in continuing diversity through the
> application of the principles of Confederation and com-
> promise, this will serve as precedent for other states in the
> world having similar population and cultural problems. It will
> be Canada's contribution to the world. Let us also remember
> that in Canada we have the world in miniature. World peace
> and order could be achieved if the principles of unity in
> continuing diversity, brotherhood, equality, compromise,
> justice and the recognition of the freedom and dignity of
> individuals and nations are honestly applied. With a rich
> background and wealth of experience as our legacy, Canadians
> of all origins, united, can look ahead into the next century with
> faith, understanding, and confidence.[68]

As an historical account Yuzyk's book is of limited value,
although it does provide a useful summary for a novice to the
subject. It is of greater value as a definition and explanation of the
role of the "Third Element" in Canadian society as understood by
one of the leading spokesmen for a multicultural Canada and a
leader of a highly vocal ethnic group.[69]

The most substantial study concerning Ukrainian Canadians
to appear during this anniversary period was *The Ukrainians in
Canada* by Olha Woycenko, the fourth volume in the Canada
Ethnica Series sponsored by the Centennial Commission and the
Canada Ethnic Press Federation.[70] Woycenko explained her
objective as follows:

> My purpose was twofold: to portray the process of integration
> into the general stream of Canadian life on the one hand, and
> the endeavours to preserve the group's identity on the other. In
> this critical documented analysis of these processes there is no
> emphasis on details or case histories; they occur only when they
> are relevant to illustrating or reinforcing the theme of my
> work.[71]

Woycenko's study paralleled Yuzyk's in that it was a plea on
behalf of cultural diversity in Canada. She addressed Canadians
in general, asking for their official recognition of cultural
pluralism, and the Ukrainian community in particular, urging it
to unite and to work co-operatively to ensure its continued
existence and growth.

A commendable reference book, well-documented, footnoted and organized, Woycenko's study was nevertheless essentially a survey. Contrary to her introductory remarks, it relied heavily on case histories and unabashedly name-dropped in reference to those individuals who achieved fame and success on a national scale. The self-laudatory approach leaves one with the impression that Ukrainians are anxious to prove their worth as a community through the achievements of selected individuals. Conspicuously absent was any mention of Ukrainian Canadians who achieved notoriety in such pursuits as crime, suggesting Woycenko was not interested in presenting a complete picture of her people.[72] Surely, if the success of a group is measured by the success of individual members, the converse must also be true. The question also arises as to whether the community can take credit for the achievements of people who are Ukrainian in name and descent only, especially when they have no affiliations with Ukrainian organizations and make their mark in fields that have nothing to do with their background. While such persons are illustrative of Ukrainian integration into Canadian society they have little or no bearing on Ukrainian-Canadian development as they are outside the community's economic, social, religious, and cultural life. The popularity of the name-dropping approach among Ukrainian-Canadian historians would suggest that a critical appraisal of the practice is necessary.[73]

In her conventional outline of Ukrainian economic progress and rate of integration Woycenko showed how the complementary activity of the peasant farmer and the professional agronomist promoted agricultural advancement. As unskilled labourers in industry, Ukrainians were initially in the lowest strata of the work force; however, individual initiative and co-operative effort soon launched many of them on the road to financial success. Ukrainian businessmen and merchants gradually replaced the Jews who had originally served the Ukrainian communities. Economic stratification within Ukrainian-Canadian society proceeded apace with entry into business and the professions. A new leadership emerged in both economic and socio-cultural spheres, and there also appeared a group of individuals who came to view their relationship to the community as one of service only. Consequently, Ukrainian-Canadian society today is as stratified as that of any ethnic group. Some strongly identify with their roots and are moulded by their ethnic sensibility; others retain their Ukrainian heritage but fully 103 participate in Canadian life. Some are ethnically alienated but securely placed within Canadian society, while still others are motivated by materialistic concerns.[74]

Moving into the field of culture, Woycenko examined the religious history of Ukrainian Canadians and concluded that the retention of the traditional forms of worship was as important to the perpetuation of a Ukrainian identity as was the preservation of language and secular customs. She observed, however, that religious divisions have precluded co-operation on such significant matters as secular education and large-scale cultural projects, and for decades have rent the community into hostile factions.[75]

In her discussion of the education of Ukrainians, Woycenko challenged the standard approach to the subject:

> ... the first years of Ukrainian settlement in Canada, when new school districts were being organized and the school buildings erected; the difficulties encountered in acquiring qualified teachers in the developing communities; the language barrier between teachers and settlers, and the problems created through misunderstandings. All these studies delve into the bilingual school system in the Prairie Provinces (especially Manitoba), the difficulties which evolved, and the ultimate abolition of this system.[76]

Contemporary writers usually reiterated the opinions of previous observers and contended that Ukrainians, fearing assimilation, were hostile to English teachers and the public schools.[77] Woycenko, on the other hand, claimed that many of the problems experienced in the early years were not peculiar to schools in Ukrainian districts, and that Ukrainians as a rule eagerly desired the education denied them in their homeland and often assumed the initiative in having a school district established. "Contrary to Young and Yuzyk's suppositions that Ukrainian immigrants were 'opposed to English schools,' the Ukrainians took advantage of the educational opportunities."[78] In the process of founding an educational system, the inspirational leadership of committed idealists and dedicated bilingual teachers was of paramount importance. With the abolition of bilingual schools, community-financed Ukrainian schools and institutes assumed the responsibility of perpetuating the Ukrainian language and culture. Lack of co-operation among the different religious and secular organizations, however, has once again been an impediment to the co-ordination of efforts to improve quality and introduce a standard curriculum.

In the realm of politics Woycenko examined the role of the Ukrainian legislator in relation to his constitutents and his ethnic group. She admitted that in many instances the image of the ethnic politician as a spokesman for his people has been overemphasized, for duty to the state has been the primary concern. Woycenko argued, however, that Ukrainian representatives have had special responsibilities when the questions of ethnicity in Canada and an independent Ukraine have been raised and debated in Canadian legislatures.

The final two chapters of *The Ukrainians in Canada* dealt with the evolution of Ukrainian-Canadian society and the future of the Ukrainian community in Canada. Woycenko noted that the peasant pioneers, lacking a definite sense of direction, had built their life in Canada on a foundation of familiar traditions, usually associated with religious observances. Preoccupation with church-building served to delay the development of secular institutions. Organization along non-religious lines did not begin in earnest until the inter-war years, when new political groups were introduced and dominion-wide networks were established. Friction within Ukrainian-Canadian society mounted as first-wave immigrants with their Canadian orientation were criticized by nationalistic newcomers. The ideology of the Ukrainian National Federation, founded in Canada in 1932 and associated with the fascist and militaristic Organization of Ukrainian Nationalists in Europe, alienated many Ukrainian Canadians, including members of the Ukrainian Self-Reliance League, which was primarily oriented to Canadian objectives.[79] Political dissension, added to the religious sectarianism of the first immigration, further divided the Ukrainian-Canadian community. Attempts to achieve unity during the inter-war years met with failure, and it took the prodding of the federal government to effect a conciliation that produced a national superstructure in 1940.

Highly critical of the inflexible constitution of the Ukrainian Canadian Committee,[80] Woycenko contended that its undemocratic practices kept many capable Ukrainian Canadians from participating in its activities:

Thus the question arises: is the Ukrainian Canadian Com-   105 mittee truly a representative body of Ukrainians in Canada and the spokesman for the whole community, which it claims to be, when many influential individuals and organizations are outside its framework. And if not, why is this inflexible system tolerated and supported by a comparatively large part of the community. One of the answers might be the *image* of "unity" and "consolidation" which has been burning the minds and hearts of Ukrainian Canadians for decades. For the sake of this image, issues are overlooked or neglected; individuals and organizations tolerate the situation as a temporary one. Eagerly they await changes in the system. The Ukrainian community fervently hopes that in time the Committee will be re-organized on truly democratic principles, and that the executive will be elected on merit only, rather than on the basis of mechanical representation of the "big five." It is hoped that in this way the Ukrainian Canadian Committee will become a truly representative, co-ordinating body, which will stand the test of time and meet the requirements of the community as a whole.[81]

Although writing as a Ukrainian Canadian concerned for the future of her ethnic group in Canada, Woycenko was not averse to criticizing the community — doing its dirty laundry in public, so to speak — as so many of her colleagues were. Her assessment of the Ukrainian Canadian Committee stands in sharp contrast to those of Veryha and Yuzyk.

Woycenko identified seven characteristic attitudes among Ukrainians in Canada. Of marginal significance were the cantonized Ukrainian Canadians, the immovable exiles still sitting on their suitcases, and those who were culturally or ethnolinguistically apathetic. Some Ukrainian Canadians favoured total assimilation with the founding races, especially the English. Among the youth the concept of "non-linguistic Ukrainianism" was gaining popularity with the idea that knowledge of the mother tongue was not indispensable to being Ukrainian. Others recommended that the Ukrainian language and culture be given the same protection and privileges as the French and the English had, and that other nationalities be similarly recognized by the government of Canada. Finally, perhaps the most common attitude was one of political loyalty to Canada compounded with ethnic loyalty to the group.[82] From these findings, Woycenko concluded: "Out of all those trends comes a surprising relevation

— despite their differences, identity as a group is more pronounced than ever. The prevailing image of a dynamic and vocal body surpasses their boldest expectations."[83]

Despite this note of optimism Woycenko saw that it was becoming increasingly more difficult to preserve that foundation of culture — language — and that ethnic alienation accompanied its loss. Ukrainian presentations to the Royal Commission on Bilingualism and Biculturalism reflected the community's concern for the future of the Ukrainian language in Canada. Woycenko contended that if cultural diversity was to be preserved in Canada, official support of languages other than French and English was essential. Yet shortcomings within the Ukrainian-Canadian community itself further jeopardized the survival of a unique cultural entity. An overemphasis on mass action — downplaying individual effort and branding nonconformists as outsiders unless identified with a particular faction — has lost to the community the services of many talented and valuable achievers. Factionalism and rivalry have encouraged the dispersion of resources and duplication of efforts, while much energy has been expended on "ephemeral action" and little on long-term projects. Finally, a lack of co-ordination and regulation (especially in soliciting funds) of activity on behalf of Ukraine's national liberation has done little to unite the community. Woycenko concluded:

> In summing up it can be stated that the perpetuation of Ukrainain cultural life in Canada is motivated by internal as well as external factors. If it is the will of Ukrainians to survive and develop as an ethno-cultural entity in Canada, the internal detrimental factors must be faced and resolved. On the other hand, if cultural diversity in the Canada of tomorrow is to prevail, it must be recognized by governments and encouraged by moral and material assistance.
>
> In both instances vision and leadership are needed.[84]

All-in-all, Woycenko provided a commendable summary of Ukrainian-Canadian achievements in various fields of endeavour and a useful sketch of the development of the Ukrainian-Canadian community to 1967. Her analysis extended to the contemporary period, noting both the responsibilities of the Canadian government to non-British and non-French groups and the strengths and inadequacies of the Ukrainian community

107

itself. In agreement with other Ukrainian-Canadian writers of her period, she underlined the need for official recognition of the Ukrainian language and culture. Unlike Yuzyk, however, who tended to be idealistic and theoretical, she was considerably more realistic and pragmatic and unafraid to chastize the community for attitudes and actions which have hindered co-operation and undermined collective effectiveness. Although Darcovich also noted the dangers facing the continued existence of a distinct Ukrainian-Canadian identity, he focused on external threats, while Woycenko stressed the internal flaws operating within the community itself.

In 1969, *Vilni Zemli/ Free Lands: The Ukrainian Settlement of Alberta,* by the popular historian James G. MacGregor, was published. A provincial history in the manner of Yuzyk's *The Ukrainians in Manitoba,* it had a much narrower perspective and lacked the scholarly quality of the senator's study. Adopting a flowery and descriptive writing style, MacGregor included imaginary conversations and played the mind-reader to determine his characters' thoughts, attitudes, and reactions. He justified this pseudo-novelistic approach by claiming that his book was intended not only for the historian but also for the lay reader. Nevertheless, he has done the historian an injustice. Although *Vilni Zemli* included numerous quotations, sources are only sporadically provided as the work is without a bibliography, footnotes, or index. As historically accurate as the facts may be, these omissions reduce the value of *Vilni Zemli* as a source of information on early Ukrainian settlement in rural Alberta from the standpoint of any serious student of Ukrainian-Canadian history. The book contains an abundance of anecdotes which bring the pioneering and immigrant experiences of Ukrainians to the personal level but in the process tends to characterize the work as a local history.

MacGregor focused on the Edna-Star settlement, which was the first Ukrainian colony in Canada and fairly typical of those that were established later. He opened with a graphic, chatty description of Ivan Pylypiw's Galician background, his 1891 journey to Canada with Wasyl Eleniak, and his role in stimulating the emigration of the first group of Ukrainian settlers who founded the colony at Edna-Star that Pylipiw eventually joined. He characterized Pylypiw as a "restless persuasive leader" who often acted before thinking; alert and intelligent; and a visionary who recognized the significance of Ukrainians arriving in Alberta "in the beginning of things," but whose vision receded when he failed to lead the great colony that he had originally planned.

Oulining the initial hardships, the progress and reversals of fortune experienced by the pioneering Ukrainian immigrants in the vicinity of Edna-Star — including long passages on specific families that were gleaned from memoirs and personal interviews — MacGregor also covered the physical expansion of the colony, its increasing prosperity, and its maturation into a structured community. He carried his account only as far as the 1920s where he continued to emphasize, in his conclusion, the material progress and the upward mobility of the illiterate peasants and second-class citizens as they advanced into the professions and full-fledged citizenship.

MacGregor quoted extensively from the journal of Theodore Nemirsky, one of the Oleskiw-sponsored immigrants who settled in Alberta. Nemirsky later achieved prominence as assistant inspector of Ruthenian schools in Alberta and as the land guide for the Dominion Land Office in Edmonton; he was noted in Ukrainian circles for harbouring Russophile sympathies and for identifying with the Russian Orthodox Church. This point undoubtedly explains why MacGregor took a Russian Orthodox point of view[85] in his lengthy discussion of the famous law suit between the Greek Catholic and Russian Orthodox factions contesting the ownership and control of a church building originally erected near Star by the Greek Catholic community.[86] He claimed that over half of the Ukrainians living in Canada desired to return to their traditional form of worship, Orthodoxy, and implied that they were only too glad to repudiate Greek Catholicism, to which they "had been forced to adhere in Galicia."[87] Clearly, MacGregor was ignorant of the role of the Greek Catholic Church in Galician society in the late nineteenth century. His outline of the religious controversy among the Ukrainians in Alberta in the first three decades of their settlement is an unfortunate example of a superficial and misguided treatment of a complex subject by one who failed to understand or appreciate the differences in attitudes, ideologies, and factions that owed their origins to conditions in Ukrainian history and the contemporary situation as it existed in Austrian Ukraine.[88]

Vilni Zemli is a credible account of the Ukrainian settlement of Alberta — in physical and material terms — from the establishment of the first colony in 1892 through the expansion outward from this nucleus in the following thirty years. Tracing how a collection of immigrants developed the features of a patterned and orderly community, it is essentially the story of homesteading pioneers and the specifics of their integration into Canadian life. No attempt was made to analyze the spiritual evolution of the Ukrainian community in this bloc or the different forces brought to bear upon it. Even the religious developments covered in the book (from a Russian Orthodox point of view) offered more in the way of fact than interpretation. As the author relied heavily on a limited number of memoirs and personal interviews, devoting lengthy passages to individual histories, *Vilni Zemli* often has the flavour of a local history that lacks both an overview and depth.

A second history concerned with Alberta Ukrainians, *The Ukrainian Pioneers in Alberta, Canada,* was published in 1970 under the editorship of Joseph M. Lazarenko for the Ukrainian Pioneers Association in Edmonton. Largely a compilation of unrelated data and approximately ninety poorly edited autobiographies and biographies of Ukrainian pioneers in Alberta, it was an amateur effort. The biographies and reminiscences varied greatly in length and quality; collectively, however, they presented a composite picture of Ukrainian immigration in all its aspects and from various points of view. Information of an analytical or introspective nature is absent, probably because of the format of the original questionnaire. However, the family histories included in the work convey the impression that while economic assimilation has been attained, social and religious associations largely remain Ukrainian.

This section was accompanied by a collection of random articles, speeches, and letters by various contributors, on education, Ukrainians in the Alberta legislature and in federal parliament, the history behind the monument erected to the Ukrainian pioneers in Elk Island National Park in 1963, the Ukrainian press in Alberta, and excerpted references to Ukrainians in the Vegreville *Observer* from 1907 to 1921. This final selection is particularly interesting as one can discern changing attitudes over the years. The newspaper came out in support of Ukrainians during World War I, when they were generally regarded as enemy aliens, although remarks by some of its correspondents were bitter; the *Observer* printed long lists of Ukrainian donations (by village and school district) to the Patriotic Fund. Written as it was in honour of Ukrainian

pioneers, *The Ukrainian Pioneers in Alberta, Canada* was

unabashedly pro-Ukrainian, emphasizing the progress made by the group despite the many obstacles to be overcome, and referring especially to the prejudice encountered as Ukrainians entered new fields of endeavour.

One final study in English-language Ukrainian-Canadian historiography merits scrutiny. In 1970 Michael H. Marunchak published *The Ukrainian Canadians: A History,* subsidized by the Centennial Commission on the occasion of the anniversary of Confederation. An English-language translation of Marunchak's Ukrainian-language works, the book suffers from sloppy editing and is plagued by things such as faulty grammar, awkward sentences, misnomers, and vacuous expressions, not to mention typographical mistakes, errors in translation and the inconsistent spelling of proper names. Nevertheless, Marunchak's history is a vast compendium of information encompassing the breadth of Ukrainian-Canadian life. An excellent and well-illustrated reference book on the social, religious, cultural, educational, political, economic, and organizational life of Ukrainians in Canada, it divided its subject into three chronological periods. *The Ukrainian Canadians* is not an impartial study, because Marunchak openly identified with the Ukrainian community. In fact, the original Ukrainian text was not intended for a general audience but for the Ukrainian group itself. This explains Marunchak's partisanship but it does not justify the overly subjective tone of his work.

The first section of *The Ukrainian Canadians* dealt with Ukrainian immigration, settlement, and development up to and including World War I. Marunchak discussed the distribution of settlers, economic progress in agriculture and labour, and the advances made in religious, educational, and cultural spheres. His own prejudices and bitterness in the matter of Anglo-Canadian treatment of Ukrainian immigrants were not disguised, and he repeatedly censured the Canadian government for failing to assist the immigrants financially and for forcing them to settle in designated areas, often on poor land. A chapter entitled "Welcome Newcomers and Racial Prejudice" continued on with Marunchak's criticism of Anglo-Saxon bigotry accompanied by glowing praise for the innate qualities of Ukrainians that enabled them to surmount all the barriers they encountered:

The indisputable fact remains that there were long years of discrimination against Ukrainians in Canada, but they, with great stoicism, tolerated it individually and collectively, and simply ignored undeserved calumniation. Denying his personal "ego" the Ukrainian settler worked out his own destiny, building up his husbandry in step with the social life in different aspects. With his blistered and calloused hands in a copious rain of sweat, often at the cost of his health and life, the Ukrainian carried on and gained some prestige due him.[89]

Marunchak's understanding of the bilingual schools question again revealed his Ukrainian partiality. Endorsing the bilingual program, he damned the Anglo-Canadian authorities for removing Ukrainian from the schools of Saskatchewan and Manitoba. On the other hand, he labelled the oft-admired situation in Alberta as "unhealthy" since government opposition to bilingualism prevented Ukrainian teachers from achieving their goals. Like other writers within the community, Marunchak envisaged the Ukrainian-English teachers as young idealists dedicated to the enlightenment of their people.

His detailed examination of the embryonic community life embraced everything from religion to culture and education. He probed the issues that arose out of religious strife; the establishment of private educational institutions; the initiation of cultural and educational work on a local level across Canada; and the first ventures into literature, publication, and the press. Recognizing the existence of an identifiable and motivated Ukrainian-Canadian community prior to World War I, Marunchak demonstrated its continued association with the Ukrainian homeland by documenting its activities on behalf of Ukrainians in Europe and its representation of Ukrainians in Canada during the First World War. Written as it was from a Ukrainian point of view, *The Ukrainian Canadians* focused on the evolution of a Ukrainian-Canadian collectivity, stressing internal development over the integration into Canadian life. Juxtaposed against the observations of Anglo-Saxons writing in the first years of immigration about ignorant Ukrainian peasants with their peculiar habits and outlandish dress, Marunchak's picture of a complex, directed, and well-organized community is a reminder of the gulf in understanding that separated Anglo-Saxon observers from the inner dynamic of Ukrainian-Canadian life.

Part Two of *The Ukrainian Canadians* covered the inter-war years, that period in Ukrainian-Canadian life which witnessed not only the creation of dominion-wide superstructures for Ukrainian-Canadian organizations and increased differentiation within the community, but also the growth of Canadian consciousness and pride as Ukrainians began to integrate and to accept Canada as their adopted motherland. Marunchak scrutinized the characteristics of the inter-war Ukrainian immigration, the Ukrainian-Canadian agencies that were formed to facilitate the influx of people, and the conflicts and tensions that accompanied the arrival of new ideologies with the political groupings they spawned. These ideological divisions were to characterize Ukrainian-Canadian life between the two wars. Marunchak approached the various religious, cultural, and political organizations that existed in the inter-war years in terms of their origin, rise, goals, orientation, activities, and leadership. He also considered the advances that were made during this period in agricultural, political, educational, cultural, religious, literary, and publishing fields. To his credit, Marunchak devoted space to the left-wing segment of the community and its historical role in Ukrainian-Canadian life; he was considerably more objective in his treatment of the left than Yuzyk had been in *The Ukrainians in Manitoba.* His acknowledgment of the existence of Ukrainain Protestants is yet another indication that his study went beyond the usual concentration on the "traditional" Ukrainian groups. Showing how concern for the fate of Ukraine in the 1920s and 1930s and support of an independent Carpatho-Ukraine in 1938-1939 helped to unite Ukrainian Canadians on a national scale, Marunchak saw the creation of the Ukrainian Canadian Committee as the climax of this second era.

World War II marked the beginning of the third era of Ukrainian-Canadian history — the era of consummation — which was distinguished by renewed patriotism for both Canada and Ukraine. Marunchak discussed the role played by Ukrainian Canadians and their associations in easing the transition for Ukrainian displaced persons emigrating to Canada. He examined the social composition of that immigration and assessed its impact on the established Ukrainian-Canadian community, noting its introduction of new political-cultural organizations and its contributions to intellectual life. Vertical and horizontal integration into Canadian society at all levels continued in the postwar years. At the same time the gradual acceptance of the concept of multiculturalism permitted the re-introduction of the Ukrainian language into the public schools and paved the way for 113 its entry into Canadian universities. Ukrainian scholars, writers, poets, artists, musicians, and performers were actively participating in both Ukrainian-Canadian and Canadian spheres. The community's continued concern for the plight of Ukrainians around the world led to the calling of a Pan-American Ukrainian Conference in 1967 (which declared itself not only the cultural but also the political representative of Ukrainians in the Americas) and the convening of the World Congress of Free Ukrainians in the same year.

Apart from being an excellent reference work on events, organizations, issues, publications, and individuals in Ukrainian-Canadian life, *The Ukrainian Canadians* also considered the influence Ukrainian Canadians have had in redefining the concept of Canadian identity. Throughout his study, Marunchak emphasized the conscious duality of the Ukrainian-Canadian community, which simultaneously attempted to integrate into Canadian society while retaining its unique cultural identity and its interest in the fate of Ukraine. This orientation Marunchak claimed, was first promoted by Ukrainian-Canadian leaders during the pioneer era. Unlike other Ukrainian-Canadian historians, the majority of whom are Canadian-born, Marunchak stressed the European outlook and interests of the Ukrainian-Canadian community over its involvement in Canadian affairs. He illustrated how the structures and attitudes of the community have always been influenced by developments in Europe and Ukraine, showing how Ukrainian Canadians reacted to various stimuli from abroad. This European orientation and pronounced personal concern for the future of the Ukrainian people has undoubtedly affected Marunchak's opinions about the situation of the Ukrainian-Canadian community within Canadian society in general. Predictably he opposed assimilation: "True enough, there were those who tried to lend to this assimilation the noble air of patriotism and Canadianization, but the new Canadians, especially the Ukrainians, who were putting a different content into Canadianization, saw this assimilation for what it was and called it 'degeneration'."[90]

Expressing his faith in the Ukrainian-Canadian community and the government's commitment to multiculturalism, Marunchak's prophecy for the future of his people in Canada was nevertheless naively optimistic:

114   If we take into consideration the conscious striving of the active

Ukrainian community to oppose the assimilation processes in
the lingual and cultural field, and the honest conviction of the
government circles that depriving the national entities of their
language and cultural values only acts to the detriment of
Canada, making it that much poorer in its spiritual content —
gaining instead only groups of "cultured" nihilists — and
finally seeing that the natural propelling force of every society
renews itself at certain intervals in future generations, as shown
by modern sociology, then we may assume that the assimilation
processes of the Ukrainian community in Canada will hardly
advance much further. On the contrary, all arguments point to
the fact that in the sphere of language and culture a turn-about-
face action, toward the past, is coming into its own. In evidence
of this we have numerous publications on the occasion of the
75th Anniversary of the Ukrainian settlement in Canada and
Canada's own Centennial celebration, amply proving that the
past not only holds interest for the authors of history books but
also for the whole society, especially the younger generation.[91]

His belief that the forces of assimilation have been checked is
questionable, especially in the light of the indifference most
Ukrainian Canadians seem to feel about their culture, and the
lack of prospects for future immigration from Ukraine to
replenish and revive the various organizations. He himself was
forced to concede that major obstacles had to be overcome if the
Ukrainian-Canadian community was to continue to develop.

In a final chapter Marunchak examined Ukrainian-Canadian
aspirations on the eve of the Canadian Centennial. Presentations
to the Royal Commission on Bilingualism and Biculturalism
reflected a dual concern for an increased sense of Canadian unity
and the preservation and growth of all nationalities in Canada.
For Ukrainian Canadians this issue was complicated by the fact
that the existence of their language and culture was being
threatened in their ancestral homeland. Marunchak concluded
his monumental history with a prediction for the future of the
Ukrainian-Canadian community:

In general we must presume that the growth of the Ukrainian
community (society) in Canada will continue, more or less,
with the same accepted form of tendencies and ambitions as has
been going on before. The Ukrainian Canadian society is a
relatively young group, filled with zest for development and

115

growth. The biggest impediment in the cultural development is the lack of the further influx of new immigrant forces, as well as the difficulty of keeping the physical ties with the culture of the motherland. The balancing medium in this case is the great psychological reaction arising, not only from the natural cultural sources, but also the continued trend of the political situation in the old country as well.[92]

In addition to a bibliography of English- and Ukrainian-language titles and a list of the patrons who sponsored the book, Marunchak's study contained a detailed index of personal names; churches, parishes and church organizations; lay organizations and co-operatives; schools and educational institutions; data related to publications; and geographical place names. The index alone indicates the vast scope of *The Ukrainian Canadians* and provides easy access to information on Ukrainian-Canadian history spanning eighty years of life in Canada.

In conclusion, a survey of the English-language literature on Ukrainian Canadians from 1946 to 1970 reveals the rapid growth and increasing sophistication of research done in the field of Ukrainian-Canadian studies. Not only has greater attention been paid to the development of the Ukrainian group in Canada (both as an identifiable collectivity and an integrated unit in Canadian society), but there has also been a consistent attempt to define the role of Ukrainian-Canadians in the evolution of a Canadian identity and the direction of Canadian development. Specialization in particular aspects of Ukrainian-Canadian life has noticeably increased and contributed towards a more comprehensive view of Ukrainian-Canadian history at all levels. This type of research will undoubtedly continue. The number of general histories has also increased, indicating a healthy and widespread interest in the Ukrainian-Canadian past.

What is still needed are more studies of specific issues in Ukrainian-Canadian development, a higher level of debate among contemporary Ukrainian-Canadian historians, the wider exchange of ideas between Anglo-Saxon and Ukrainian historians so as to synthesize views within both groups, and more penetrating study and analyses of various developments to better determine the motives and attitudes behind events. An infusion of fresh ideas and insights could only advance Ukrainian-Canadian historiography. There are too few comprehensive examinations of specific occurrences or significant issues. Some of the shorter works have focused on particular developments, but published monographs have thus far, with the exception of Kaye's *Early Ukrainian Settlements in Canada,* provided general accounts of Ukrainian-Canadian progress while neglecting the disciplined study of particular phenomena.

Conclusion

During the past seventy years, English-language literature on Ukrainians in Canada has reflected the evolving concepts of Canadian identity and nationhood as they considered the impact of non-British and non-French minorities. The major studies have assessed the Ukrainian Canadians progressively in terms of Anglo-conformity and assimilation, the "melting pot" and the "mosaic," and the current understanding of "Canadian" as multiculturalism in a bilingual framework. These stages in development have consistently determined the orientation of English-language works on Ukrainians in Canada, although a recent trend initiated primarily by Ukrainian-Canadian historians, has focused attention on particular aspects and events in the community's life without considering them in the context of these larger questions. The emphasis on overviews of Ukrainian-Canadian history interpreted in terms of Canadian objectives and development still persists, but serious scholarship and increased specialization in this field of study have added repute and credibility to Ukrainian-Canadian historiography. The time has come for more detailed study and analysis to be conducted on the specific issues, incidents and episodes and important figures of Ukrainian-Canadian history.

In the early years of Ukrainian life in Canada, the Ukrainian community was fairly easily defined by bloc settlements, and Ukrainian-Canadian history was generally understood to mean the economic, political, cultural, and educational development of these districts. The organized Ukrainian community, predicated on European-Ukrainian associations and movements, was only one facet of Ukrainian life in these areas. However, with the increasing integration of Ukrainians into all spheres of Canadian life and the almost complete assimilation of their cultural distinctiveness, the history of most Ukrainian Canadians becomes no different than that of any other group in Canada.

Consequently, research into the economic, political, and social development of Ukrainian Canadians, while remaining valid for the early decades of Ukrainian settlement in Canada, loses significance as a continuing fruitful field of activity with assimilation and integration on a larger scale. At the same time, however, research into organized community life grows in importance.

In the future the question of what constitutes Ukrainian-Canadian history will require discussion and re-definition. Should a Canadian of Ukrainian descent — regardless of the level of his ethnic awareness — who achieves fame as a hockey superstar, a geophysicist, a world wheat champion, or a virtuoso pianist, automatically be considered within Ukrainian-Canadian history? Does having Ukrainian ancestry or a Ukrainian name necessarily mean that an individual's accomplishments illustrate the success and progress of the entire ethnic group when his cultural, social, and religious associations are those of Canadian society? Is he making a distinctly Ukrainian-Canadian contribution to Canadian life? On the other hand, can Ukrainian-Canadian historiography be legitimately restricted to the study of the organized community?

These and other problems require careful consideration, as assimilation and intermarriage continue to diminish the number of Ukrainian Canadians who actively propagate Ukrainian cultural traditions and instill in their children a concern for the fate of the Ukrainian nation in Europe. The promotion and preservation of the Ukrainian language and culture in Canada is slowly becoming the task of an ever-shrinking minority generally identified with the organized Ukrainian-Canadian community. Present trends would seem to suggest that Ukrainian-Canadian historiography in the future will focus on this minority as both the guardian and visible manifestation of a Ukrainian-Canadian subculture within Canadian society.

It would be unjustifiable to conclude, however, that the prospects for Ukrainian-Canadian historiography are bleak. There is a vigorous interest in the development of Ukrainians in Canada and research is being undertaken with ever-broadening horizons. Ukrainian-Canadian historiography is a firmly established discipline, with works in languages other than Ukrainian and English, and publications outside Canada to attest to its existence beyond ethnic and national boundaries. Lastly, its activity is illustrative of contemporary work in the realm of social and intellectual history in Canada in general.

Bibliographies pertaining to the Ukrainian-Canadian experience exist either as separate publications restricted to that ethnic group or as part of general Canadian ethnic bibliographic collections in which the Ukrainian-Canadian section constitutes only a chapter of the whole. In both instances they catalogue research activity on the Ukrainian group in Canada and the popular, literary, and scholarly output of the community itself.

The first annual bibliography to include Ukrainian-Canadian titles appeared in the summer issue of the *University of Toronto Quarterly* under "New Canadian Letters," renamed in 1960 "Publications in Other Languages." Begun in 1937 by Watson Kirkconnell,[1] this feature reviews selected works published in Canada in a given year, beginning with 1935, in languages other than French and English. The survey concentrates on Ukrainian-Canadian prose, poetry, and drama.

In 1951 the Ukrainian Free Academy of Sciences initiated the annual publication of *Slavica Canadiana* as a subsection of Slavistica.[2] The first part of each issue is a selected bibliography — compiled on a yearly basis with supplementary listings for previous years — of books and pamphlets published in or relating to Canada. The works are arranged alphabetically by author in categories such as religion, literature and literary criticism, biographies and memoirs, and history. Part Two consists of book reviews, commentaries, and reports, and includes reviews of any new publications on Ukrainians in Canada. From the Ukrainian point of view, however, the importance of *Slavica Canadiana* as a bibliographic reference has been eclipsed by a second UVAN publication, *Ukrainica Canadiana.*

Since 1954 *Ukrainica Canadiana* has been published annually in a two-part edition.[3] Part One, incorporated into its similarly
organized equivalent of *Slavica Canadiana,* is a selected

bibliography of Ukrainian books and pamphlets published in a given year in or relating to Canada, with supplementary listings for previous years. A broad cross-section of publications varying in type, quality, and length, and ranging from historical monographs to annual reports and letters, are included in the bibliography. As with *Slavica Canadiana,* many of the items reflect nothing of Ukrainian life in Canada. Part Two was originally a guide to the current Ukrainian press in Canada, but in 1956 it began to note only those Ukrainian-Canadian newspapers and periodicals introduced in the previous year. *Ukrainica Canadiana* has also printed three bibliographic essays.[4]

In 1954 the Canadian Citizenship Branch of the Department of Citizenship and Immigration launched the publication of an annual bibliography entitled *Research on Immigrant Adjustment and Ethnic Groups.* A supplementary volume in 1955 covered unpublished theses completed between 1920 and 1953 in this field. In 1960 this annual bibliographic series was succeeded by a periodic publication of the Economic and Social Research Branch. The first three volumes, published in 1960, 1962, and 1964, were entitled *Citizenship, Immigration and Ethnic Groups in Canada: A Bibliography of Research Published and Unpublished Sources.* They respectively covered the years from 1920-1958, 1959-1961, and 1962-1964. The fourth volume was published in 1969 by the Department of Manpower and Immigration under the title *Immigration, Migration and Ethnic Groups in Canada: A Bibliography of Research 1964-1968.* This selected bibliography is essentially a consolidation of the former series on immigrant adjustment and ethnic groups. Entries are organized according to a detailed subject coding system, with a comprehensive listing followed by sections for each ethnic group. The different ethnic groups have been intentionally arranged in order of numerical strength in Canada so as to show the relationship between the size of a group and the quantity of research conducted on it. The section on Ukrainians comprises primarily English- and Ukrainian-language publications, theses and works in progress, with a brief description of the contents or an author's argument. Unlike *Slavica Canadiana* or *Ukrainica Canadiana,* it does not include works published in Canada on Ukrainian affairs abroad.

The first number of Volume I of the *Canadian Ethnic Studies Bulletin* in 1969 carried three Ukrainian-Canadian

Frances Swyripa

bibliographies compiled by Alexander Malycky: "University Research on Ukrainian Canadians: A Preliminary Check List of Dissertations and Theses," "Ukrainian Canadian Periodical Publications: A Preliminary Check List," and "A Preliminary Check List of Studies on Ukrainian Canadian Literature: General Studies." In collaboration with Orysia Prokopiw and Alexander Royick, Malycky produced a fourth index, "Ukrainian Canadian Creative Literature: A Preliminary Check List of Authors and Pseudonyms." The first issue of Volume II, published in 1970, carried supplements to university research on Ukrainian Canadians and Ukrainian-Canadian periodicals. Malycky and E. Verchomin Harasymiw expanded the earlier compilations on Ukrainian-Canadian creative literature with the addition of preliminary check lists of imprints and specific studies. Sources have been credited and English, Ukrainian and other language titles are presented alphabetically by author, or by title in the case of periodicals, with minimal bibliographic information. The check lists do not claim to be comprehensive.

In reaction to the federal governments's official sanction of multiculturalism, the Ontario Department of the Provincial Secretary and Citizenship commissioned a bibliography of the literature on Canadian ethnic groups. The resultant work by Andrew Gregorovich, *Canadian Ethnic Groups Bibliography,*[5] attempts to cover a broad area and is consequently incomplete and exclusive. A general section on themes that range from human, cultural, and civil rights, language, assimilation, and integration; through the press and literature, immigration, and demography; to the Mosaic and the Melting Pot and American ethnic groups; precedes that on individual Canadian ethnic groups. Seventy-eight Ukrainian-Canadian titles are listed, the majority in the English-language, followed by other bibliographic data and a brief description of the contents and merit of each work.

This survey of Ukrainian-Canadian bibliographies has omitted unpublished compilations, Ukrainian titles that are part of general Canadian or regional bibliographies, and special studies[6] in restricted areas. Nevertheless, the major works have been recorded to indicate the availability of Ukrainian-Canadian bibliographic sources, the extent of development of this branch of Ukrainian-Canadian scholarship, and the contents and structure of such works.

122

Notes

Introduction

1. In 1972 Y.W. Lozowchuk and H. Radecki presented a paper entitled "Slavs in Canada: Selected Observations on the Literature that Deals with Polish and Ukrainian Canadians" to a Symposium on Race and Ethnic Relations in Canada at the Annual American Anthropological Association Meeting held in Toronto. A preliminary work, it indicated the descriptive and analytical literature available on the two groups, assessed its reliability, and noted recurring themes and issues, sources of data, and neglected but relevant areas of study. The study was conducted topically, outlining significant trends in specific areas, but made no attempt to evaluate critically the concepts, methodology, or data of individual works, or the progressive development of Ukrainian-Canadian historiography.

Chapter I

1. Particularly in this chapter Ukrainian, Ruthenian, and Galician will be employed interchangeably, the latter two designations representing the contemporary terms for the Slavic immigrants from eastern Galicia in the Austro-Hungarian Empire. Ruthenian referred solely to Ukrainians while Canadians frequently applied Galician indiscriminately to all East Europeans and it came to acquire definite derogatory connotations.
2. *Annual Report of the Department of the Interior* (Ottawa, 1899),17.
3. Among the most detailed descriptions of conditions in Ukrainian settlements through the eyes of resident Anglo-Saxon teachers are two unpublished letters in the W.M. Martin Papers (pp. 19163-68 and pp. 19423-31) at the Saskatchewan Archives, Saskatoon. The second letter by Elsie M. Bishop, "Some of my Experiences as a Teacher Among the New Canadians," is especially perceptive.
4. Foremost among these studies are Armand Boni, C.Ss.R., *Pioniers in Canada: De Belgische in de Provincies Quebec, Manitoba en Saskatchewan* (Brussels, 1945) and Emelien Tremblay, C.Ss.R., *Le Pere Delaere et L'Eglise ukrainienne du Canada* (Berthierville,

Quebec, 1961). French-Canadian interest in Ukrainians continued beyond the period of Roman Catholic missionary activity in the Ukrainian colonies. In 1945 a French-language doctoral dissertation, "Le status canonique des ukrainiens catholiques du rit ruthene au Canada" by Louis-Eugene Belanger, was submitted to Laval University.

5. For example, Achilles Delaere, a Belgian Redemptorist priest serving among Ukrainians at Yorkton, Saskatchewan, wrote a pamphlet, *Memorandum on the Attempts of Schism and Heresy Among the Ruthenians (commonly called "Galicians") in the Canadian Northwest* (Winnipeg, 1909), to encourage young Canadian Catholic clerics to go into the Ukrainian mission field to secure the Ukrainians for the Catholic Church, especially in light of Protestant proselytizing. Catholicism and not Canadianization motivated his concern.

6. For a concise statement of the position of the Presbyterian Church in Canada and its clergy on the issue, see Rev. W.D. Reid, Rev. H.A. Berlis, and Rev. M.C. Kinsale, "The Non-Anglo-Saxons in Canada — Their Christianization and Nationalization," papers contained in *Addresses Delivered at the Presbyterian Pre-Assembly Congress, held in Massey Hall, Toronto, Saturday, May 31st, to Wednesday, June 4th, 1913, with Reports of Committees* (Toronto, 1913), 119-34.

7. One of the more ambitious ventures was the creation of the Independent Greek Church under the auspices of the Presbyterian Church in Canada, which financed and supervised the movement. Initially enjoying spectacular popularity among Ukrainians as it utilized Ukrainian priests and the familiar Eastern liturgy and helped alleviate the spiritual vacuum in which Ukrainians found themselves, its demise was rapid when the Presbyterian Church exerted pressure to adopt Protestant teachings and discard the ritual. In 1913 the Independent Greek clergy were admitted into the ministry of the Presbyterian Church in Canada but their congregations failed to follow.

8. Especially valuable in this regard and for depicting developments chronologically in the various Presbyterian and Methodist missions are the annual reports and letters on Galician, Austrian, and Ruthenian work contained in the *Acts and Proceedings of the General Assemblies of the Presbyterian Church in Canada* from 1898 to 1925, and the *Missionary Bulletin* of the Methodist Church. In addition, in 1905 a Ukrainian-language newspaper, *Ranok,* was founded and assisted financially and editorially by the Presbyterian Church. It soon published articles on farming and gardening, social and moral reform, and national life as well as on religion.

9. A.J. Hunter, *The Kobzar of the Ukraine; Being Select Poems of Taras Shevchenko* (Teulon, 1922).

10. See P. Cundy, *A Voice from Ukraine* (Winnipeg, 1932), a collection of the poetry of Ivan Franko; *Ivan Franko: The Poet of*

Western Ukraine, ed. by Clarence A. Manning (New York, 1948); and *Spirit of Flame: A Collection of the Works of Lesya Ukrainka* (New York, 1950).

11. This is well illustrated by the case of the Independent Greek Church, whose history has received relatively little scrutiny in subsequent publications by the Presbyterian and United churches. For example, Rev. E.H. Oliver, writing in 1932, devoted one paragraph to Presbyterian mission work among Ukrainians and concluded tersely: "In the end the experiment failed." See *His Dominion of Canada: A Study in the Background, Development and Challenge of the Missions of the United Church of Canada* (Toronto, 1932), 198-99.

12. H.A. Kennedy, *The Book of the West* (Toronto, 1925), 142-43. This portion of the book was written in 1905, following a visit by Kennedy to western Canada to view the changes since his first journey in 1885.

13. The article also discussed Ruthenian immigration to Canada and the remarkable material progress and adaptability shown by Ukrainians. Its extreme optimism no doubt reflected the Liberal policy of the *Winnipeg Free Press,* owned by Clifford Sifton, Minister of the Interior in Sir Wilfrid Laurier's Liberal cabinet to 1905. It was republished in the *Yorkton Enterprise* (Sept. 9, 1909), and later reprinted with an introduction by V.J. Kaye as "The Ruthenians" in *Canadian Slavonic Papers,* Vol. I (1968), 96-99.

14. It is impossible not to generalize when examining the treatment of Ukrainian settlers in travelogues. Although the remarks are succinct and disparate, certain trends dominate. For a list of those travel diaries considered in this survey, consult the bibliography.

15. A notable exception was Agnes C. Laut, *The Canadian Commonwealth* (Indianapolis, 1915), chap. 7, "The Coming of the Foreigner," 111-26. Though she praised immigrants from Scandinavia, Iceland, and Germany, her condemnation of the foreigner from southern and eastern Europe was vituperative. She claimed he possessed the potential to contaminate Canadian national ideals; encouraged political corruption; promoted crime as one formerly restrained by a "soldier's bayonet" knew not how to handle freedom; and although earning less than his Canadian counterpart would become the wealth and power of the future as he spent very little. In spite of her vicious attack on foreigners and their threat to Canadian ideals, Laut opposed their exclusion on the grounds that from the national point of view Canada required them for manual labour. At the same time, their assimilation was essential. Primary responsibility lay with the school, where the efforts of too many teachers to "manufacture men and women out of mud" (125) had gone unrecognized.

16. J.H. Hardy, "The Ruthenians in Alberta," *Onward,* Nov. 1, 1913, 346.

17. *Annual Report of the Department of the Interior,* 17.

18. See also "A Russian Wedding in Alberta" in which Elston

recounted the religious and secular ceremonies associated with a Ukrainian wedding. Ukrainian weddings were popular topics among Anglo-Saxon writers, probably because of their novelty and because they were one prominent occasion in which an Anglo-Saxon in a Ukrainian community could participate, however vicariously, and hence be able to describe. Apart from simply depicting the wedding rituals, female teachers in particular deplored what they termed "child marriages" in which the child bride was married against her wishes or without her consultation to a man much older than she. Criticisms of the quantities of home brew consumed and the "traditional" fight that concluded Ukrainian weddings were common.

19. Elston's mistaken use of "Russian" when referring to the Ruthenians can be easily explained. Her descriptions of Ukrainian religious services were exclusively those of the Orthodox Church and at that time the Russian Orthodox Church in America was responsible for the establishment of Orthodox missions among Ukrainian settlers in Canada. No doubt this association, assisted by the failure of the Russian Church to differentiate between the Russian and Ruthenian peoples, confused Elston.

20. J.A. Carmichael, Superintendent of Home Missions for Manitoba and the North-West, spoke of this need in his report contained in the *Acts and Proceedings of the Thirty-Second General Assembly of the Presbyterian Church in Canada* (1906):

> ... the treatment of the Galicians in their own homes has decided advantages for the missionary, for he has the opportunity of teaching those in the home how to take care of the sick, and of winning the confidence of the homes thus visited, and of laying the foundation of future work. From a missionary standpoint the ordinary medical practice has decided advantages over hospital work (13).

Although the Presbyterian Church was motivated by the desire to provide Ukrainians with educational opportunities and medical care, such programs were considered to be the first and necessary step towards more aggressive evangelical work, as they served to counteract traditional prejudices and fears.

21. R. Connor, *The Foreigner: A Tale of Saskatchewan* (Toronto, 1909), 14.

22. This is substantiated by the British and American editions of the novel published in London and New York under the title, *The Settler: The Story of a Ukrainian Youth*. See S.K. Jain's compilation, *Saskatchewan in Fiction: A Bibliography of Works of Fiction about Saskatchewan and Fiction Written by Saskatchewanians* (Regina, 1966), 4; and B.B. Peel, *A Bibliography of the Prairie Provinces to 1953* (Toronto, 1956), 224.

23. Connor, *The Foreigner,* 87-88.

24. *Ibid.,* 160.

25. See *ibid.,* 253-55 for the arguments for and against Galician

immigration and education as articulated by French and Brown at
their first meeting. This passage is crucial to understanding
Connor's own beliefs regarding the assimilation of non-Anglo-
Saxons, for the author was openly sympathetic to the Presbyterian
clergyman, Brown.

26. *Ibid.,* 371-72.
27. For example, see J.M. Gibbon, *Canadian Mosaic: The Making of a
Northern Nation* (Toronto, 1938), 276-77:

> The vivacious and graceful dancing of a Polish group at the New
> Canadian Folk-song and Handicraft Festival held in Winnipeg
> in 1928, had a marked influence on the attitude taken by Anglo-
> Saxons towards the foreign born in that city. When that festival
> was being organized, I was told quite frankly by a number of
> those whom I met there that the CPR was doing the wrong thing
> in encouraging these people to retain their old customs. In the
> course of conversation, it usually developed that the critics were
> influenced by a novel written 20 years before by Ralph Connor,
> the popular Canadian novelist, entitled *The Foreigner,* a
> somewhat lurid melodrama of the shack-town which had grown
> up on the skirts of this mushroom city. . . .

Gibbon persuaded Connor, his friend, to attend the Polish
performance, after which Connor remarked: "I always looked on
the Poles as husky, dirty laborers whose chief entertainment was
drink, but these are delightful, cultivated people. I feel that I have
done them an injustice in my book. What can I do to make
amends?" *Ibid.,* 277. If Gibbon's report is accurate, Connor had not
bothered to become better acquainted with the Slavs in Canada in
the twenty years following the publication of *The Foreigner.*
28. J.S. Woodsworth, *Strangers Within our Gates or Coming
Canadians* (Toronto, 1909), 4.
29. *Ibid.,* 114.
30. Ford drew a distinction between the comparative standards of the
Galicians and Bukovinians: "Illiterate and ignorant as are the
Galicians, the Bukovinians are even more so. . . . It is probable that
if an analysis were made of the nationality of those charged with
crimes, the result would show a far greater number of Bukovinians
than Galicians." *Ibid.,* 135. Ford's observation is interesting and
one only wishes that he had elaborated on his statement. It perhaps
reflects the Galician stereotype of the Bukovinians as "un-
sophisticated and bucolic, rural hayseeds." See J.C. Lehr,
"Ukrainian Houses in Alberta," *Alberta Historical Review,* Vol.
XXI (Aug. 1973), 14.   In his discussion of Ukrainian pioneer
cottage architecture in Alberta, Lehr maintained that traces of
these traits could be detected in Bukovinian houses, while the
Galician houses were often smaller and more conservative,
reciprocally reflecting the Bukovinian stereotype of the Galicians as
thrifty and miserly.
31. Woodsworth, *Strangers Within our Gates,* 136.

32. *Ibid.,* 136-37.
33. *Ibid.,* 289.
34. During World War I, Woodsworth, a pacifist, continued to emphasize the necessity of recognizing the assets of the different immigrants — ambition, a capacity for patient labour, rich cultures, and often a patriotism needed by Canada because it had inherited the liberty for which other nations had had to fight. He also criticized both patriotic and religious "Canadianizing" institutions for undermining the immigrants' foundation of tradition: "Destroy filial respect and reverence and love of the homeland and what do we have to work on? . . . If ever we in Canada attain a national ideal, it must be big enough — Catholic enough — to give a place to the highest and best which each class of immigrant brings to this country." J.S. Woodsworth, "Nation Building," *University Magazine,* Vol. XIII (Feb. 1917), 85-99.
35. Woodsworth, *Strangers Within our Gates,* 305. A spirit of religious independence manifested in the rise of the Independent Greek Church was a further indication of the "leaven of Western civilization" acting upon the Ruthenians.
36. J.T.M. Anderson, *The Education of the New Canadian: A Treatise on Canada's Greatest Educational Problem* (London and Toronto, 1918), 135.
37. For his information on the European background of the Slavic peoples, Anderson relied on an American publication: E.G. Balch, *Our Slavic Fellow Citizens* (New York, 1910).
38. These qualities were not attributed to the Slavs by Anderson himself but were gleaned from Professor Steiner's *The Immigrant Tide: Its Ebb and Flow.* See Anderson, 60-61.
39. *Ibid.,* 114.
40. *Ibid.,* 152.
41. The Public Archives of Canada has one copy and a second is among the Martin Papers in the Saskatchewan Archives Office, Saskatoon.
42. J.S. Woodsworth, "Ukrainian Rural Communities," Report of Investigation by Bureau of Social Research, Governments of Manitoba, Saskatchewan, and Alberta (Winnipeg, 1917), 4.
43. *Ibid.,* 6.
44. The treatment of the Ukrainians in Canada (from 1914 to 1921) as enemy aliens by the government and the Canadian public, and the inter-relationship of immigrants, politics, and the war during those years has been examined by J.A. Boudreau, "The Enemy Alien Problem in Canada, 1914-1921" (unpublished Ph.D. dissertation, University of California, Los Angeles, 1965). See also J.A. Boudreau, "Western Canada's 'Enemy Aliens' in World War One," *Alberta Historical Review,* Vol. XII (Winter 1964), 1-9.
45. The attacks on Bishop Budka prompted the Roman Catholic Church to rally publicly to his defence. See Catholic Truth Society of Canada, *Vindication of Bishop Budka: Full Record of Investigation: A String of Unfounded Charges: Judge Paterson's Summary* (Toronto, 1919), 6.

46. E.H. Oliver, speaking in 1915 against bilingual education in Saskatchewan, voiced his alarm at the activities of Ukrainian nationalists, particularly in light of the Ruthenians' potential as a political force and their movement into the political arena on the municipal and provincial levels. See *The Country School in Non-English Speaking Communities in Saskatchewan* (originally delivered as an address to the Saskatchewan Public Education League in 1915 and subsequently published in pamphlet form), 15-18. In this pamphlet Oliver also presented a sympathetic summary of Ukrainian history in terms of national oppression and the debt owed Ukraine by western Europe for bearing devastation by the Mongols "while other more fortunate nations beyond that living hedge developed and prospered" (16).

47. Anticipating the interest Anglo-Canadians were to show (in the inter-war years) in the folksongs and handicrafts of New Canadians was the translation and annotated publication by Florence R. Livesay, journalist and author of *Songs of Ukraina with Ruthenian Poems* (London, Paris, and Toronto, 1916). The book consisted of selected pagan, wedding, historical, Cossack, robber and chumak songs, and poems by Shevchenko, Rudansky, Vorobkievich, and Fedkovich. It closed with a translation of the Ukrainian national anthem. Livesay was assisted in her endeavour by Paul Crath (Pavlo Krat), a Ukrainian student radical who escaped to Canada imbued with social democratic and atheistic ideals but who underwent a spiritual transformation in 1915 which led to his ordination into the Presbyterian ministry in 1917. In his introduction to Livesay's translation, Crath painted an idyllic picture of Ukraine. Crath and Livesay also collaborated on an article, "Religion of Ancient Ukraine — in light of Archeology and Folklore," published in *Scientific American Supplement,* Vol. 85 (Feb. 1918), 114-15. In 1940, Livesay translated and published Hryhory Kvitka's novel *Marusia.* The introduction by Lord Tweedsmuir stressed the need for Canadians to become more familiar with the culture of the East Europeans residing in Canada.

Chapter II

1. For an indication of British and Canadian conceptions of the Canadian identity, see Sir Robert Falconer, "What is Implied in the Word Canadian," *English Review,* Vol. XLI (Oct. 1925), 595-604; and W.B. Hurd, "Is There a Canadian Race?" *Queen's Quarterly,* XXXI (1928), 615-27. Falconer named the attachment to Great Britain and resistance to absorption by the United States as the two salient factors fostering Canadian unity. Hurd, on the other hand, examined the evolution of a distinctly Canadian nationality from the varied racial strains in the country in the light of the psychological emergence of a Canadian nation following the war.

He concluded that the melting pot had not yet yielded its product, for no Canadian race existed. Although considerable racial and cultural fusion had already occurred, biological amalgamation would require more time.

2. M. Elston, "Ruthenians in Western Canada. I. Public Schools," *Onward,* April 12, 1919.

3. M. Elston, "Our Own Slav Problem: Ukrainians in Canada," *Graphic,* Aug. 9, 1919.

4. F. Heap, "Ukrainians in Canada: An Estimate of the Presence, Ideals, Religion, Tendencies, and Citizenship of Perhaps Three Hundred Thousand Ukrainians in Canada," *Canadian Magazine of Politics, Science, Art and Literature,* Vol. LIII (1919), 43.

5. See in particular C.G. Young, "Report for Board of Home Missions and Social Service for Year Ending 1919 — Report on Non-British Mission Work in Northern Saskatchewan," *Acts and Proceedings of the Forty-Sixth General Assembly of the Presbyterian Church in Canada* (1920), 33-41. Young summarized Ukrainian history from the founding of Kieven Rus' in the ninth century through the devastation and oppression by eastern hordes and avaricious neighbours, to acknowledging the great recuperative powers and inner strength of the Ukrainian people, and expressing hope for the fate of the fledgling Ukrainian Republic. He also outlined Ukrainian immigration to Canada and the material and spiritual progress achieved with the help of the Presbyterian Church and British Christian teachers.

6. C.G. Young, *ibid.* (1919), 32.

7. W.H. Sedgewick, *ibid.* (1924), 9.

8. The Medical Director of the Canadian National Committee for Mental Hygiene adopted the stance that although Canada needed immigrants, those mentally defective only constituted a drain on the state and in no way contributed beneficially to Canadian development. Hence, a wiser immigration policy than that in force prior to 1918 was an absolute necessity. See W.G. Smith, *A Study in Canadian Immigration* (Toronto, 1920), 8-15.

9. *Ibid.,* 382-83.

10. W.G. Smith, *Building the Nation: The Churches' Relation to the Immigrant* (Toronto, 1922), 109.

11. *Ibid.,* 111.

12. F. Yeigh, "New Canadians Making Good," *Canadian Magazine of Politics, Science, Art and Literature,* Vol. LIX (1922), 227-35.

13. J.W. McAllister, "The Rural School as a Community Centre: A Discussion Dealing with the Problem of the Assimilation of New Canadians in Western Canada" (unpublished M.Sc. thesis, University of Alberta, 1925), 3.

14. P.H. Bryce, *The Value to Canada of the Continental Immigrant* (Ottawa, 1928), 13. This was probably an allusion to the remark by the Anglican bishop of Saskatchewan, George Exton Lloyd, that this class of immigrant were "dirty, ignorant, garlic-smelling, non-preferred continentals." Lloyd made his comment in a letter dated

June 29, 1928, imploring the Protestant ministry of western Canada to oppose continental immigration in large numbers. See M. Luchkovich, *A Ukrainian Canadian in Parliament: Memoirs of Michael Luchkovich* (Toronto, 1965), 61-62. Bryce elsewhere condemned the official Anglican stand against those people whose accomplishments he had just enumerated.

15. Bryce, 44.
16. R. England, *The Central European Immigrant in Canada* (Toronto, 1929), x.
17. *Ibid.,* 6. Italics in original.
18. *Ibid.,* 56-59.
19. *Ibid.,* 72.
20. For example, England contended that there were few books and no newspapers, musical instruments or organized meetings. That such was not the case has been aptly illustrated by Ukrainian-Canadian historians researching developments in the inter-war years. For an indication of the quantity, variety, and circulation of Ukrainian-language press publications in this period, and an account of the network of national and local organizations of various orientations, see M.H. Marunchak, *The Ukrainian Canadians: A History* (Winnipeg, 1970), 470-98 and 374-424 respectively.
21. Actually, the Ukrainian peasant family had a definite matriarchal element, for women enjoyed undisputed responsibility for the home and garden while husbands dominated the world outside. Wife-beating did occur on occasion — usually provoked by intoxication — but it was not a socially accepted practice. Finally, in an agricultural society, marriage was not exclusively a matter of choice for the young couple, since the transfer of family property was also involved. A marriage agreement therefore required a consensus of opinion among both sets of parents and the bride and groom. Peasant societies engaged in subsistence farming also demand the dedication of husband, wife, and children, and the initial stage of Ukrainian rural life in Canada preserved this traditional orientation.
22. England, *The Central European Immigrant in Canada,* 89-95.
23. *Ibid.,* 134.
24. *Ibid.,* 165.
25. *Ibid.,* 175. At one point, England did state that the problem of assimilation could be reduced to the question of how to absorb the immigrant without losing the best in his heritage, but he nowhere indicated what he considered to be worth preserving. He favoured the standardization of outlook, customs, and attitudes brought about by the use of a common language and shared experiences in Canada, leaving few areas where the non-Anglo-Saxon could preserve facets of his European character and inheritance.
26. *Ibid.,* 211.
27. It is indicative of the partial success of Protestant efforts among Ukrainians that Hunter could cite few Ukrainian converts to Presbyterianism at the same time that the school, home, and hospital were being favourably received.

28. A.J. Hunter, *A Friendly Adventure: The Story of the United Church Mission Among New Canadians at Teulon, Manitoba* (Toronto, 1929), 106.
29. *Ibid.*, 44.
30. *Ibid.*, 54.
31. *Ibid.*, 36, 38.
32. *Ibid.*, 102-3.
33. G.E. Reaman, "Canadianization of the Foreign-Born," *Canadian Magazine of Politics, Science, Art and Literature,* Vol. LIX (Oct. 1922) 449.
34. The latter part of this statement requires qualification, for the Ukrainian national historical experience was viewed as a contributing factor in the development of certain traits in the Ukrainian character potentially valuable to Canada — a democratic tradition in Cossackdom and a devout patriotism to the Ukrainian nation nurtured through centuries of oppression bore promise of a similar loyalty to Canada.
35. K.A. Foster, *Our Canadian Mosaic* (Toronto, 1926), 7.
36. *Ibid.*, 135.
37. E.L. Chicanot, "Moulding a Nation," *Dalhousie Review,* Vol. IX (1929), 233.
38. Gibbon, *Canadian Mosaic,* viii.
39. For example, see Rev. D.G. Ridout, "European Sources of Non-Anglo-Saxons in Canada," *Canadian Geographical Journal,* Vol. II (March 1931), 201-23, which contended that any study of Canadian life required a careful consideration of the sources of its civilization, but mentioned Ukrainians only in passing; also L. Hamilton, "Foreigners in the Canadian West," *Dalhousie Review,* Vol. XVII (1938), 448-60; and W. Murray, "Continental Europeans in Western Canada," *Queen's Quarterly,* Vol. XXXVIII (Winter 1931), 63-75, which discussed signs of progress in education, agriculture, arts, handicrafts, and citizenship as observed through the Community Progress Competitions conducted in 1930 among continental Europeans by the colonization department of the CNR.

40. C.H. Young, *The Ukrainian Canadians: A Study in Assimilation* (Toronto, 1931), ix-xi.
41. Young's summary of Ukrainian history was a scholarly review and not an attempt to recount the nation's folk history. A well-organized presentation, it made continued confusion and ignorance on the part of Anglo-Canadians inexcusable. Later writers relied heavily on Young for their information on the historical background of Ukrainians.
42. *Ibid.*, 199.
43. *Ibid.*, 207-8.
44. Young's observation is interesting, particularly when one considers that school teachers, too, commented on the prevalence of lying and petty thievery and the lack of shame on the part of the culprits. The Ukrainian peasant had long felt no guilt about pilfering from

the estate of a landlord. The wife of a Polish landlord in pre-Revolutionary Russian Ukraine commented in her memoirs on the peasant's sense of property. The essence of her observations was that in the peasant's mind all property belonged either to God or to the master. Fruit in the orchard, hay in the haystack, timber in the forest, and grain on the threshing floor belonged to God. It was no sin or disgrace to take these. However, the manor house and its contents were the master's domain, and anyone caught stealing therein was roundly condemned by his peers. See Maria Dunin-Kozicka, *Burza od Wschodu: Wspomnienia z Kijowszczyzny 1918-1920* (Storm from the East: Memories from the Province of Kiev 1918-1920) (Warsaw, 1929), 23-24.

45. Young, 282.

46. *Ibid.,* 308.

47. R. England, *The Colonization of Western Canada: A Study of Contemporary Land Settlement (1896-1934)* (London, 1936), 308.

48. *The Ukrainian Canadians* was not the only work to discuss the history of Ukraine. In 1932, disturbed by the failure of Canadians to study such an important component of national life, A.J. Hunter presented a paper to the Historical and Scientific Society of Manitoba entitled "The Ukrainians: Their Historical and Cultural Background." Hunter's address was later abridged and published in series III (10), 1955, of the *Transactions of the Historical and Scientific Society of Manitoba.*

49. At times, however, England's professional integrity could be questioned. For certain material he cited Young as his source, while in other instances, information was borrowed almost *verbatim* from Young without credit. For example, compare pages 73 to 75 of Young with pages 203 to 205 of England regarding the identification and description of the twelve Ukrainian bloc settlements from southeastern Manitoba to Alberta, or page 15 of Young with page 206 of England concerning Ukrainian historical background. There is no doubt that England admired *The Ukrainian Canadians,* as indicated in his review of it in the *Canadian Historical Review,* Vol. XII (1931), 209.

50. England, *The Colonization of Western Canada,* 214-15.

51. J.M. Deverell, "The Ukrainian Teacher as an Agent of Cultural Assimilation" (unpublished M.A. thesis, University of Toronto, 1941), 112.

52. L. Bercuson, "Education in the Bloc Settlements of Western Canada" (unpublished M.A. thesis, McGill University, 1941), 173-74.

53. C.M. Bayley, "The Social Structure of the Italian and Ukrainian Immigrant Communities in Montreal, 1935-1937" (unpublished M.A. thesis, McGill University, 1939), 7-8.

54. Byrne included the French translation of Michael Hrushevsky's abbreviated history of Ukraine in his bibliography; all other entries on Ukrainian historical background were listed under "Magazine Reviews."

55. T.C. Byrne, "The Ukrainian Community in North Central Alberta"

(unpublished M.A. thesis, University of Alberta, 1937), 5.

56. *Ibid.,* 83.

57. Byrne defined assimilation as the absorption of a lesser group by a group greater in numbers, culture, and prestige. Although he did not elaborate, this suggests little of the process of "give and take" put forward by other writers of his period.

58. Byrne excluded the adherents of the Russian Orthodox Church and Ukrainian Labor-Farmer Temple Association, the former because of their lack of Ukrainian identification and the latter because of their internationalism.

59. What Byrne referred to as the National Union was known in Ukrainian as Ukrainske Natsionalne Obiednannia (UNO) and in English as the Ukrainian National Federation. Where he acquired the term National Union is not stated.

60. Byrne, "The Ukrainian Community in North Central Alberta," 98.

61. Kirkconnell's interest in the ethnic groups residing in Canada predated World War II. In 1935 he published *Canadian Overtones,* an anthology of Canadian poetry — originally written in Icelandic, Swedish, Norwegian, Hungarian, Italian, Greek, and Ukrainian — translated and edited by himself with biographical, historical, critical, and bibliographic notes. He hoped this volume would acquaint English Canadians with this significant contribution to Canadian literature and foster their appreciation of newer Canadians as human beings, besides encouraging in the latter a pride in their ethnic origins. See, in particular, "Ukrainian-Canadian Poetry," *Canadian Overtones* (Winnipeg, 1935), 76-104.

During World War II, J.M. Gibbon made a similar attempt at enlightenment in a paper presented to the Royal Society of Canada in which he argued for the popularization of the national literatures of all the ethnic groups in Canada through selected translations of representative works. With such a "secular Bible," Canadians of all nationalities could become acquainted with the hearts and minds of their fellow citizens and so promote unity, mutual understanding, and assimilation. Gibbon suggested that Section II of the Royal Society of Canada take on the task of translation as its contribution to post-war reconstruction. See "A Secular Bible for a New Canada," *Transactions of the Royal Society of Canada,* Vol. XXXVI, 3rd series, 1942, sec. ii, 93-100.

62. See also W. Kirkconnell, "The European Canadians in Their Press," *Canadian Historical Association Report* (1940), 85-92, in which he discussed the ethnic press primarily as an indication of the degree of assimilation of European Canadians, but also viewed it as a propagandistic tool reflecting native movements that were potentially disturbing to Canada. He maintained, however, that four-fifths of the foreign-language press in Canada was hostile to Hitler and loyal to the Dominion.

63. A scathing criticism of Kirkconnell's treatment of the Ukrainian question in *Canada, Europe, and Hitler* was written by an inter-war Ukrainian immigrant to Canada, M.I. Mandryka, and published by the Canadian Ukrainian Educational Association under the title

The Ukrainian Question: Remarks to Prof. Watson Kirkconnell's book: "Canada, Europe and Hitler" (Winnipeg, 1940). Mandryka purported to correct Kirkconnell's "errors and misleading assertions" regarding Ukrainian history, the nationalist movement, the future Ukrainian state, and the antagonistic Ukrainian factions (nationalist and communist) in Canada. However, Mandryka's own "facts" and statements were in many instances inaccurate or open to question, and his entire interpretation of the points under discussion was decidedly subjective and nationalistic in tone.

64. W. Kirkconnell, *Our Ukrainian Loyalists: The Ukrainian Canadian Committee* (Winnipeg, 1943), 23.

65. See also W. Kirkconnell, *Our Communists and the New Canadians* (originally delivered as an address before a meeting of the Canadian Club at Toronto, Feb. 1, 1943). This pamphlet does not deal with Ukrainians exlusively but indicates Kirkconnell's hostile attitude towards the Communist Party of Canada and its objectives.

66. In a pamphlet entitled *An Appeal for Justice: The Case of the Seized Properties of the Ukrainian Labor-Farmer Temple Association* published in 1944, the Civil Liberties Association of Toronto sympathetically reviewed the treatment of the ULFTA from its banning by the Canadian government and the seizure of its property in 1940 to its reinstatement to legal status in 1943, when that property not destroyed or sold cheaply to rival Ukrainian organizations was restored. As the ULFTA received no compensation for the property that was destroyed and only the low sums paid by the purchasers of their holdings, the Civil Liberties Association hoped to arouse Canadian public opinion to a condemnation of the injustice perpetrated on the ULFTA and thus spur the Canadian government to offer some form of redress. With this objective in mind the pamphlet was understandably emotional in tone, but it does provide a summary of the material fortunes of ULFTA in centres across Canada during World War II.

67. Davies made every effort to establish and play up the relationship between the Ukrainian National Federation and the terrorist and fascist OUN in Europe, including Nazi sympathies, and the pro-German policy of the United Hetman Organization, contending that both organizations were directed from Berlin.

68. See J.W.S. Grocholski, ed., *Preliminary Survey on Integration of the Canadian Racial, Cultural and Nationality Groups from the Standpoint of Canadians of Various Origins other than British or French* (Toronto, 1944), which examined integration for the benefit of Canadian unity when confronted with the inevitable social, economic, and political crises that would follow victory. While basically theoretical and general in its orientation, the pamphlet did use Ukrainian Canadians for its illustrations. It concluded that the non-British and non-French elements, while sharing common citizenship, would first have to enter the Anglo-Saxon sphere of Canadian life and only then intermingle to create the Canadian nation of the future. The third element was a potentially binding force in the relationship between the two founding races.

Chapter III

1. A valuable account of life on a railway gang has been provided by an American of Slavic extraction, Ely Culbertson, in *The Strange Lives of one Man: An Autobiography* (Chicago, Philadelphia, Toronto, 1940), 270-73. Involved in the construction of the Grand Trunk Pacific Railway approximately fifty miles from Edmonton, Culbertson recounted the exploitation of Ukrainian labourers, whom he described as "naive, trusted, bearded giants," and his own role as a strike leader and intermediary between them and their Anglo-Saxon employers.

2. V. Lysenko, *Men in Sheepskin Coats: A Study in Assimilation* (Toronto, 1947), 80.

3. See Young, *The Ukrainian Canadians,* 146-47.

4. Lysenko, *Men in Sheepskin Coats,* 117-18.

5. In a strangely naive review of *Men in Sheepskin Coats* in the *Canadian Historical Review,* Vol. XXIX (1948), 88, J.M. Gibbon, who had done some study of Ukrainian history, either failed to detect the communist bias in Lysenko's book or did not deem it worthy of comment. W. Kirkconnell also reviewed *Men in Sheepskin Coats* (see *Opinion,* July 1948), at which time he unmasked its communist interpretation.

6. Lysenko, *Men in Sheepskin Coats,* 148.

7. *Ibid.,* 203-4.

8. *Ibid.,* 302.

9. See Panteleimon Bozhyk, *Tserkva ukraintsiv v Kanadi. Prychynky do istorii ukrainskoho tserkovnoho zhyttia v brytiiskii dominii Kanady, za chas vid 1890-1927* (Churches of the Ukrainians in Canada: Contributions to the History of Ukrainian Religious Life in the British Dominion of Canada from 1890-1927) (Winnipeg, 1927). An account of religious developments among Ukrainian immigrants in the first three decades of the twentieth century, Bozhyk's history was written from the Catholic point of view which he adopted when he left the Orthodox priesthood to serve as a priest in the Ukrainian Greek Catholic Church.

10. At first the Ukrainian intelligentsia was composed almost exclusively of school teachers. Yuzyk's discussion of the role of education in the Ukrainian districts is particularly interesting in the light of the repeated assertions of Anglo-Saxon writers that Anglo-Canadian teachers bore the brunt of the responsibility of inculcating their immigrant students with Canadian citizenship ideals. He commented: "To the pioneer Ukrainian-English teacher, above all, must be attributed the progress that was made in the Ukrainian settlements not only in education but in cultural, economic and political affairs." It was he who had "gradually formed out of an unenlightened and indifferent peasant a Canadian citizen conscious of his responsibilities to his adopted country and proud of his Ukrainian heritage." P. Yuzyk, "Ukrainian Greek

Orthodox Church of Canada (1918-1951)" (unpublished Ph.D. dissertation, University of Minnesota, 1958), 104.

11. J. Skwarok, "The Ukrainian Settlers in Canada and their Schools with Reference to Government, French-Canadian, and Ukrainian Missionary Influences 1891-1921" (unpublished M.Ed. thesis, University of Alberta, 1958), ix.

12. The inclusion of a picture of the first car in Minburn, Alberta, in the chapter on the history of Ukrainian immigration to Canada is a typical example. Similarly, Skwarok's supplement on Ukrainian literature, while informative, was extraneous to the topic of the Ukrainian settlers and their schools.

13. To cite one example Skwarok inexplicably quoted two different figures for the total Ukrainian immigration to Canada before World War I, at one point stating that 150,000 Ukrainians had entered the Dominion during this period, but later giving the number as 200,000. See Skwarok, "The Ukrainian Settlers in Canada and their Schools," ix and 11.

14. *Ibid.*, 11.

15. *Ibid.*, 125.

16. Skwarok stated: "A simple rustic folk forming the backbone of the nation, lovers of the soil, but having no soil on which they could produce those necessary economic fruits, lovers of their nation and conscious of their glorious historical past, they were continually harassed by foreign governments to the point where they were forbidden to speak their own language under pain of fines and imprisonment." *Ibid.*, 7.

17. For example, Skwarok implied that such restrictions as the requirement of permission to marry (see *ibid.*, 3) lasted until 1848. He also stated: "The Pan [landlord] was his judge, master, taxer, and final administrator. He also had patrimonial rights over the poor serf which meant that he could punish him corporally, and there were no laws limiting the measure of this punishment." *Ibid.*, 4. The impression he gave was that this situation, too, continued until 1848. Such, however, was not the case. Joseph II had secured minimal economic and civil rights for the peasantry by the end of the eighteenth century, when it became possible to marry without the landlord's permission and one could appeal to the state administration in matters of abuse.

18. See J.G. MacGregor, *Vilni Zemli/ Free Lands: The Ukrainian Settlement of Alberta* (Toronto, 1969), 8-9. MacGregor quoted almost the entire passage by Skwarok on conditions as they existed prior to 1848, not only retaining Skwarok's mistaken assertions (see footnote 17) but also applying them to Galicia and Bukovina in 1870.

19. O.S. Trosky, "A Historical Study of the Development of the Ukrainian Greek Orthodox Church of Canada and its Role in the Field of Education (1918-1964)" (unpublished M.Ed. thesis, University of Manitoba, 1965), 1. See Ivan L. Rudnytsky, "The Ukrainians in Galicia under Austrian Rule," *Austrian History*

Yearbook, Vol. III, Part 2 (1967), 394-429, which clearly shows the falsity of Trosky's statement.

20. See M.R. Nebel, "Rev. Thomas Johnson and the Insinger Experiment," *Saskatchewan History,* Vol. XI (1958), 1-16, for a similarly laudatory account of the work of the Presbyterian Church and its representatives, notably Johnson, among Ukrainians at Insinger, Saskatchewan. The article concisely portrays the activities of an Anglo-Saxon group working in an Ukrainian community to assimilate the residents into Canadian life not through religious conversion but by education and good example.

21. M. Wenstob, "The Work of the Methodist Church among Settlers in Alberta up to 1914, with Special Reference to the Formation of Congregations and Work among the Ukrainian People" (unpublished B.D. thesis, University of Alberta, 1959), 124. It is interesting to note that in 1959 Wenstob still referred to Ukrainians by the outdated term, "Galicians."

22. See M. Stefanow, "A Study of Intermarriage of Ukrainians in Saskatchewan" (unpublished M.A. thesis, University of Saskatchewan, 1962), for an indication of the degree of inter-marriage in that province (between 1951 and 1961) interpreted as a measure of assimilation. Stefanow noted a decline in endogamy among Saskatchewan Ukrainians during this period and concluded that "Ukrainians in Saskatchewan are losing their identity as a group, or conversely, Ukrainians are taking on the prevailing Western Canadian culture which is dominated by the English speaking." *Ibid.,* 96. Similar trends probably apply to other provinces with large Ukrainian populations.

23. See H. Piniuta, "The Organizational Life of Ukrainian Canadians, with Special Reference to the Ukrainian Canadian Committee" (unpublished M.A. thesis, University of Ottawa, 1952), xxix-xxx.

24. See also A. Royick, "Ukrainian Settlements in Alberta," *Canadian Slavonic Papers,* Vol. X (1968), 278-97, which established the districts of origin of the Ukrainians in the various communities of Alberta and the corresponding Ukrainian dialects spoken in these localities; and Z.S. Pohorecky and A. Royick, "Anglicization of Ukrainian in Canada between 1895 and 1970: A Case Study of Linguistic Crystallization," *Canadian Ethnic Studies Bulletin of the Research Centre for Canadian Ethnic Studies,* Vol. I (1969), 141-219, which viewed the Anglicization of Ukrainian not as a symptom of social disintegration, language decay, or acculturation, but as a healthy and humorous response to a foreign environment that equipped the language for survival in its new surroundings.

25. See also V.J. Kaye-Kysilewskyj, "Political Integration of Ethnic Groups: The Ukrainians," *Revue de l'Universite d'Ottawa,* Vol. XXVII (Oct.-Dec., 1957), 460-77; and "Golden Jubilee of Participation of Ukrainians in Political Life in Canada," *Ukrainian Quarterly,* Vol. XIX (1963), 167-70, which recapped Kaye's previous accounts of Ukrainian integration into Canadian political life by listing elected Ukrainian representatives at various levels of

government (stressing Ukrainian-Canadian "firsts" in this sphere).
26. P. Yuzyk, *The Ukrainians in Manitoba: A Social History* (Toronto, 1953), ix.
27. A review of *The Ukrainians in Manitoba* by Watson Kirkconnell in the *Canadian Historical Review,* Vol. XXXV (1954), 61, suggested that Yuzyk's summary of Ukrainian history was not without its bias:

> The only possible hint of bias comes in the historical summary (p. 18) of Eastern European warfare in 1918-20 where it is assumed that Lviv was Ukrainian in character (instead of being a fiercely Polish-minded island in a sea of Ukrainian peasantry) and where no mention is made of the joint Polish-Ukrainian campaign against the Bolsheviks in the spring of 1920; but this distortion by omission may perhaps be blamed on the hazards of compressing the complex events of two years into half a page.

Interestingly enough, Kirkconnell did not criticize Yuzyk's fervent anti-communism, though he did remark that Yuzyk had shown "clearly that the frequent public impression that most Ukrainian Canadians are pro-communist is completely false."
28. Yuzyk, *The Ukrainians in Manitoba,* 96-97.
29. *Ibid.,* 111-12.
30. See also P. Yuzyk, *For a Better Canada* (Toronto, 1973), a collection of selected speeches delivered in the Canadian Senate and at banquets and conferences across Canada.
31. Yuzyk, *The Ukrainians in Manitoba,* 212.
32. See P. Krawchuk, "Ukrainian Image in Canadian Literature," *Tribute to our Ukrainian Pioneers in Canada's First Century,* 28-42, for a discussion, coloured by the Communist convictions of the author, of the Ukrainian figure as he has appeared in English-language Canadian fiction.
33. See M.I. Mandryka, *History of Ukrainian Literature in Canada* (Winnipeg, 1968), for an account of the development of Ukrainian-Canadian literature, concentrating on Ukrainian-language novelists and poets writing on Ukrainian, Ukrainian-Canadian, and universal themes. It also examined the scholarly work of both Ukrainians and non-Ukrainians in Ukrainian and Ukrainian-Canadian studies. Organized basically into three divisions determined by the three phases of Ukrainian immigration and life in Canada, the book provided a particularly useful biographical sketch and discussion of the more important individuals in each period.
34. For example, Landash was portrayed as insensitive and inhuman in his attempt to force Lilli to marry an elderly, coarse, but prosperous farmer, yet he refused to participate in a village witch hunt because he did not want to alienate the school teacher — Ian MacTavish — whom he admired and respected. That MacTavish strongly opposed Lilli's arranged marriage did not seem to disturb Landash.

35. V. Lysenko, *Yellow Boots* (Toronto, 1954), 263. Lysenko's over-riding concern for the peasant turned labourer was undoubtedly prompted by her left-wing class consciousness. Interestingly enough, a fellow communist, Peter Krawchuk, admonished Lysenko for her failure to deal with the problem of exploitation and discrimination:

> In my opinion Vera Lysenko idealizes the life of Ukrainians in Canada, ignores the exploitation of immigrants by agents, mortgage companies, banks, storekeepers and agricultural machinery companies. She ignores the political deception of immigrants by both conservative and liberal politicians. She says nothing of the humiliation of national pride through racial discrimination which was, in the period of the novel, prevalent in Canada.

See footnote 32, P. Krawchuk, "Ukrainian Image in Canadian Literature," 37. The question raised by Krawchuk's criticism embraces that of the function of literature in society.
36. Lysenko, *Yellow Boots,* 201.
37. *Ibid.,* 297.
38. *Ibid.,* 301.
39. I. Kiriak, *Sons of the Soil* (Toronto, 1959), 90.
40. *Ibid.,* 302.
41. The original Ukrainian manuscript was published in 1958 under the title *Moi pionerski pryhody v Kanadi* (My Pioneer Experiences in Canada).
42. That Fry harboured communist sympathies is corroborated by the fact that one of the three forewords was contributed by J. Chitrenky, secretary of the Association of United Ukrainian Canadians.
43. O.R. Fry, *My Heritage from the Builders of Canada* (New York, 1967), 103.
44. See Appendices A and B for Luchkovich's reply in the House of Commons (1929) to Lloyd's letter and the ensuing debate; and for his speech (1931) on the Polish pacification of eastern Galicia.
45. Luchkovich, *A Ukrainian Canadian in Parliament,* 59-60.
46. Andre Laurandeau died on June 1, 1968, and in his place Jean-Louis Gagnon was appointed to serve as co-chairman with Davidson Dunton.
47. E.D. Wangenheim, "The Ukrainians: A Case Study of the 'Third Force'" in *Nationalism in Canada* (Toronto, 1966), 73.
48. *Ibid.,* 83.
49. *Ibid.,* 90.
50. See also V.J. Kaye, "Dr. Joseph Oleskow's Visit of Canada, August-October, 1895," *Revue de l'Universite d'Ottawa,* Vol. XXXII (Jan.-March 1962), 30-40.
51. *Pro vilni zemli* (About Free Lands) — published in Lviv in 1895, prior to Oleskow's visit to Canada — was written to dissuade prospective Ukrainian immigrants from emigrating to Brazil and to

persuade them to choose Canada. Intended as a guide for potential immigrants, the pamphlet provided an accurate description of conditions in Canada — climate, size, population, government, schools — based on information solicited from the Canadian government. Oleskow promised a more detailed report on his return from his inspection tour. This was subsequently contained in his second pamphlet, *O emigratsii* (About Emigration), published after his return to Galicia.

52. As it was, Canadian government officials soon noted the difference between those immigrants selected by Oleskow, who brought some money with them, and those procured by steamship agents in Europe, who often arrived destitute.

53. V.J. Kaye, *Early Ukrainian Settlements in Canada 1895-1900: Dr. Josef Oleskow's Role in the Settlement of the Canadian Northwest,* (Toronto, 1964), 131.

54. For example, see *ibid.,* 278-317, regarding the establishment of the colonies in the Yorkton and Rosthern regions. Although the government strove to settle Ukrainians at sites that it had selected, it also at times materially assisted in the erection of the first hut and the initial breaking of the soil, and provided outside work for Ukrainians.

55. *Ibid.,* 376.

56. Volume III of *Slavs in Canada* was not published until 1971 and hence is outside of the scope of this survey. It contained two articles on Ukrainian Canadians: "Ethnic Identification and Attitudes of University Students of Ukrainian Descent" by Bohdan Bociurkiw and "Languages in Conflict: Ukrainian and English" by E.N. Burstynsky.

57. The representatives from Nebyliw stressed the contrast between the historical conditions that forced the residents of the village to emigrate and the favourable situation in contemporary Nebyliw under progressive Soviet rule.

58. Association of United Ukrainian Canadians and Workers' Benevolent Association of Canada, *Tribute to our Ukrainian Pioneers in Canada's First Century,* 48.

59. *Ibid.,* 73.

60. W. Veryha, "The Ukrainian Canadian Committee: Its Origin and War Activity" (unpublished M.A. thesis, University of Ottawa, 1967), xv-xvi.

61. W. Darcovich, *Ukrainians in Canada: The Struggle to Retain their Identity* (Ottawa, 1967), iii.

62. *Ibid.,* 38.

63. Yuzyk was consistent in his anti-communist bias: "Fortunately, the communist movement has declined rapidly after the last war, thanks to the work of the loyal Ukrainian organizations, particularly the Ukrainian National Federation and the co-ordinating body, the Ukrainian Canadian Committee. The communist movement among the Ukrainian Canadians is relatively very weak today, but must be watched as it operates under innocent-sounding names." P. Yuzyk, *Ukrainian Canadians: Their*

Frances Swyripa

Place and Role in Canadian Life (Toronto, 1967), 43-44.

64. *Ibid.,* 47.
65. *Ibid.,* 51.
66. *Ibid.,* 89-90.
67. See *ibid.,* 91.
68. *Ibid.,* 92.
69. See also P. Yuzyk, "75th Anniversary of Ukrainian Settlement in Canada," *Ukrainian Review,* Vol. XIV (Spring 1967), 81-86, which stressed Ukrainian success in agriculture and politics with the usual name-dropping and enumeration of "firsts" in both fields, Ukrainian-Canadian service in the armed forces during the two world wars, and the cultural contribution of Ukrainian Canadians. Yuzyk's final section on the mission of Ukrainian Canadians reiterated his message in *Ukrainian Canadians: Their Place and Role in Canadian Life.*
70. Other volumes in the series examined the Indians and Eskimos, Icelanders, Germans, Lithuanians, Italians, Poles, and Japanese.
71. O. Woycenko, *The Ukrainians in Canada* (Winnipeg, 1967), xiv-xv. See also O. Woycenko, *Canada's Cultural Heritage: Ukrainian Contribution,* originally delivered as an address to a symposium on Canada's Cultural Heritage at the Annual Meeting of the Provincial Council of Women, held in Winnipeg in November of 1963 (Winnipeg, 1964); and O. Woycenko, "Ukrainian Contribution to Canada's Cultural Life. Report Presented to the Royal Commission on Bilingualism and Biculturalism" (Winnipeg, 1965), for similar treatments of related material. The organization of Woycenko's presentation to the Royal Commission resembled that of *The Ukrainians in Canada* but focused primarily on cultural, religious, educational, and individual contributions to Canada.
72. It is interesting to recall that several major Anglo-Saxon works dealing with Ukrainian Canadians stressed such negative attributes, although this emphasis, like that of Ukrainian-Canadian historians, tended to be lop-sided.
73. The members of the Royal Commission on Bilingualism and Biculturalism in Canada faced this question in initially determining what constituted the "cultural contribution of the other ethnic groups," but failed to come up with a conclusive definition. See *Report of the Royal Commission on Bilingualism and Biculturalism: The Cultural Contribution of the Other Ethnic Groups* (Ottawa, 1970), Book IV, Foreword.
74. Woycenko, *The Ukrainians in Canada,* 66.
75. Woycenko introduced an interesting concept into Ukrainian-Canadian religious history. Stating that Ukrainian fear of Latinization by the predominantly French missionaries of the Roman Catholic Church working in the early years of Ukrainian settlement was one factor behind the establishment of the Ukrainian Greek Orthodox Church, she suggested that these experiences and fears were responsible for the negative attitude of that church towards French Canadians and the Quiet Revolution

in Quebec, which was labelled as a Catholic movement. The Ukrainian Greek Catholic Church, however, tends to be more sympathetic to French Canada. See *ibid.*, 84.

76. *Ibid.*, 86.

77. To illustrate her point, Woycenko cited W.L. Morton, *Manitoba: A History* (Toronto, 1957), 311.

78. Woycenko, *The Ukrainian in Canada*, 92-93. In *The Ukrainians in Manitoba* (145) Yuzyk had stated: "In the early period the Ukrainians themselves were in many instances opposed to English schools and English teachers, on the ground that these were instruments of assimilation employed to wipe out their nationality and culture." How Woycenko could justify her own criticism in the light of Ukrainian opposition to English teachers as recorded, for example, in the *Annual Reports* of the Department of Education in Alberta — where bilingualism was not introduced — is not stated.

79. Here Woycenko criticized Yuzyk's account (in *The Ukrainians in Manitoba*) of inter-war developments in the political affiliations of Ukrainian Canadians, for his failure to note that the Ukrainian National Federation was a Canadian branch of the Organization of Ukrainian Nationalists. See Woycenko, *The Ukrainians in Canada*, 200. Yuzyk was among the founders of the youth sector of the Ukrainian National Federation, and in the light of its later embarrassment for its pro-fascist and pro-Hitler stance until the outbreak of World War II, probably deliberately omitted mention of this connection. See W. Kirkconnell, *Canada, Europe, and Hitler* (Toronto, 1939), 142-44, for a discussion of the position of the Ukrainian National Federation on the eve of World War II.

80. The constitution of the Ukrainian Canadian Committee decrees that executive positions to the presidium are to be delegated not according to democratic election on merit, but according to representation of the major member organizations.

81. Woycenko, *The Ukrainians in Canada*, 214-15.

82. *Ibid.*, 218-19.

83. *Ibid.*, 219.

84. *Ibid.*, 222.

85. Only in the second last chapter did MacGregor admit that "to some extent the entries in his [Nemirsky's] journal must be considered as presenting only one side of the story." Even then, however, he did not acknowledge that his earlier account of developments, based on Nemirsky's journal, would therefore have been similarly biased. See MacGregor, *Vilni Zemli*, 248.

86. In 1904 Justice Scott handed down his decision in favour of the Greek Catholic supporters. It was upheld in 1905 by the Supreme Court of the North-West Territories. In 1906, however, the Supreme Court of Canada awarded the Russian Orthodox faction the property and in 1907 the Lords of the Privy Council passed final judgment in favour of the Russian Orthodox faction.

87. *Ibid.*, 169.

88. See also footnote 18, notes to chap. III, regarding MacGregor's

confused account of contemporary economic and social conditions in Galicia.

89. Marunchak, *The Ukrainian Canadians,* 77.
90. *Ibid.,* 716.
91. *Ibid.,* 721.
92. *Ibid.,* 730.

Appendix

1. Watson Kirkconnell also published specific Ukrainian-Canadian bibliographies, including "Ukrainian Canadians" in *Canadian Forum* (Jan. 1934) and "Ukrainian Canadian Literature" in *Opinion* (Sept.-Oct. 1947).
2. J.B. Rudnyckyj was the sole editor of *Slavica Canadiana* from 1952 to 1956. From 1957 to 1969 he edited the multilingual series with the co-operation of individuals specializing in different branches of the Slavic family. Over the years they have included D. Sokulsky (Ukrainian), L.J. Strakhovsky, V. Turek (Polish), C.N. Bedford (Russian), J. Kirschbaum (Slovakian), I. Avakumovic (Serbo-Croatian), H.F. Chanal (Russian), and T.W. Krychowski. In 1956 the Canadian Association of Slavists began to assist UVAN in the publication of *Slavica Canadiana* and in 1962 the Polish Institute of Canada became the third co-publisher.
3. To 1963, Part One was compiled by J.B. Rudnyckyj and Part Two by D. Sokulsky. In 1964 Rudnyckyj became the sole compiler. He was succeeded in 1971 by Z. Horbay and O. Woycenko.
4. J.B. Rudnyckyj, "Ukrainian Canadian Bibliography," *Ukrainica Canadiana 1962,* No. 10 (Winnipeg, 1963), 6-10, and "Ukrainian Canadian Press 1903-1963: A Bibliographic Survey," *Ukrainica Canadiana 1963,* No. 11 (Winnipeg, 1964), 5-9; and Danylo Lobay, "Ukrainian Press in Canada," *Ukrainica Canadiana 1966,* No. 14, translated and revised by Olenka Negrych (Winnipeg, 1967), 17-32.
5. Andrew Gregorovich, *Canadian Ethnic Groups Bibliography: A Selected Bibliography of Ethno-Cultural Groups in Canada and the Province of Ontario* (Toronto, 1972).
6. Robert Klymasz, for example, has done extensive work in the field of Ukrainian-Canadian folklore. Among his publications in this area is a 463-item bibliography, "A Bibliography of Ukrainian Folklore in Canada, 1902-1964," *Anthropology Papers,* No. 21 (Ottawa, National Museum of Canada, 1969).

Bibliographic Note

In a study of this nature it is sometimes revealing if individual contributions to the literature on Ukrainians in Canada are considered within the context of the background and outlook of the author. Although knowledge of a particular author is not essential to understand or appraise his work, it can be helpful in many ways. It can clarify why a person was prompted to write on Ukrainians or why he adopted a certain bias towards them. A writer's qualifications — be they academic, artistic or experiential — may enhance or undermine his credibility as a commentator on the subject of Ukrainian-Canadian history. Being familiar with his other activities also helps to place his interest in Ukrainian-Canadians into perspective.

With these considerations in mind, the bibliography has been arranged so as to provide a brief biographical note on each author following the bibliographic citation of his work. Where applicable (for those individuals on whom information was available) the source has been indicated. The bibliography has been organized chronologically and corresponds with the chapter divisions in the text; within this framework works have been grouped according to genre, with entries made alphabetically by author.

Bibliography

I. 1896 - 1918

Books and Pamphlets

Anderson, James T.M. *The Education of the New Canadian: A Treatise on Canada's Greatest Educational Problem.* London and Toronto, J.M. Dent & Sons, 1918. 271 pp.

    Ontario born, Anderson (1878-1946) received his B.A. in 1911, his LL.B. in 1913, and his M.A. in 1914 — all from the University of Manitoba. In 1918 he was granted a D. Paed. from the University of Toronto. Inspector of schools at Yorkton, Saskatchewan, at the time he wrote *The Education of the New Canadian,* he was appointed director of education for New Canadians in Saskatchewan in 1918. He was especially vigilant about education in Ukrainian settlements. Chosen leader of the Saskatchewan Conservative Party in 1924, Anderson was elected to the provincial legislature in 1925 and from 1929 to 1934 served as premier of Saskatchewan. In his later years he was superintendent for the School of the Deaf in Saskatoon.

    Source: W.S. Wallace, ed., The Macmillan Dictionary of Canadian Biography, 3rd ed. (Toronto, Macmillan, 1963), 13.

Brooke, Rupert. *Letters from America.* New York, Charles Scribner's Sons, 1916.

    Brooke (1887-1915), an English poet, in 1913 undertook a year's journey to Canada, the United States, and the South Seas. The first thirteen chapters of *Letters from America* were originally written for the *Westminster Gazette* while the remaining two appeared in the *New Statesman* shortly after the outbreak of war. Minimally edited, the collection was republished posthumously in *Letters from America.* Ukrainians are discussed in chapter X, "Outside" (111-20).

Cameron, Agnes D. *The New North: Being Some Account of a Woman's Journey Through Canada to the Arctic.* New York and London, D. Appleton & Co., 1910.

    Cameron (1863-1912), educationalist and writer, taught for eighteen years in British Columbia schools and was elected school trustee for Victoria in 1906. In 1908 she embarked on a 10,000-mile journey from Chicago to the Arctic Ocean *via* Athabasca, Great Slave Lake, and the Mackenzie River, returning by way of the Peace River and Lesser Slave Lake. She recorded her trip in *The New North*. Her pride in her British ancestry was undisguised. Ukrainians are discussed in chapter II, "Winnipeg to Athabasca Landing" (19-32).

    Source: Macmillan Dictionary of Canadian Biography, 103.

Delaere, Achilles. *Memorandum on the Attempts of Schism and Heresy Among the Ruthenians (commonly called "Galicians") in the Canadian Northwest.* Winnipeg, West Canada Publishing Co., Ltd., 1909. 42 pp.

    The Belgian Redemptorist Fr. Achilles Delaere (1868-1939) emigrated to Canada in 1899 to serve the spiritually leaderless Ukrainian Greek Catholics. He established a mission at Yorkton, Saskatchewan. Active in obtaining a Greek Catholic bishop for the Ukrainians in Canada, Delaere eventually received permission to transfer personally from the Latin to the Eastern Ruthenian rite. During his visit to Canada in 1910, Count Andrii Sheptytsky — the Ukrainian Metropolitan of Lviv — was so impressed with Delaere's work among Ukrainians that on his return to Galicia he founded an Eastern-rite branch of the Congregation of Our Most Holy Redeemer.

    Source: G.W. Simpson, "Father Delaere, Pioneer Missionary and Founder of Churches," *Saskatchewan History,* Vol. III (Winter 1950), 1-16.

Fraser, John F. *Canada As It Is.* 2nd ed. London, New York, Toronto and Melbourne, Cassell & Co., Ltd., 1911.

    An Englishman, Fraser toured Canada for the purpose of seeing first-hand its people, topography, and potential for development. The first edition was published in 1905. Ukrainians are discussed in chapter IX, "Winnipeg: The City of the Plains" (100-13) and chapter XII, "The North-Wester: A Britisher with all the Improvements" (141-52).

Gordon, Charles W. [Ralph Connor]. *The Foreigner: A Tale of Saskatchewan.* Toronto, Westminster Co., Ltd., 1909. 384 pp.

    The Rev. C.W. Gordon (1860-1937) was educated in his native Ontario, receiving his B.A. from the University of Toronto in 1883 and his D.D. from Knox College (Toronto) in 1906. He was ordained into the ministry of the Presbyterian Church in Canada in 1890. Following three years of service as a missionary to miners and lumbermen in the N.W.T., he served as pastor to St. Stephen's Presbyterian Church in central Winnipeg from 1894 until his death. During World War I Gordon was a chaplain in the Canadian Expeditionary Force and in 1922 was elected moderator of the Presbyterian Church in Canada. He became a fellow of the Royal Society of Canada in 1904 and in 1935 was awarded the C.M.G. Under the pseudonym of Ralph Connor, he achieved great popularity as a novelist writing on various Canadian themes.

    Source: Macmillan Dictionary of Canadian Biography, 270-71.

Kennedy, Howard A. *New Canada and the New Canadians.* London, Horace Marshall & Son, 1907. Chap. VI: "Middle Alberta and the Galicians" (123-30).

    Journalist and author, Kennedy (1861-1938) emigrated to Canada from England in 1881. A staff member of the Montreal *Daily Witness* from 1881 to 1890, he was its war correspondent during the second Riel Rebellion. In 1890 Kennedy returned to England but visited Canada periodically until 1912, when he settled here permanently and worked as a freelance journalist. *New Canada and the New Canadians* was the result of a 1905 tour of western Canada to ascertain changes since 1885. From 1929 until his death, Kennedy was the national secretary of the Canadian Authors' Association. Ukrainians are discussed in chapter VI, "Middle Alberta and the Galicians" (123-30).

    Source: Macmillan Dictionary of Canadian Biography, 362.

McEvoy, Bernard. *From the Great Lakes to the Wide West: Impressions of a Tour Between Toronto and the Pacific.* London, Sampson Low, Marston & Co., Ltd., 1902.

    McEvoy (1842-1932), journalist and author, left his native England in 1888 to work for the Toronto *Mail and Empire. From the Great Lakes to the Wide West* consisted of descriptive letters originally written for the *Mail and Empire* while journeying through western Canada. In 1901 McEvoy transferred to the Vancouver *Province.* Ukrainians are discussed in chapter VII, "First Impressions of Winnipeg" (65-74) and chapter X, "Edmonton and the North Country" (100-13).

    Source: Macmillan Dictionary of Canadian Biography, 450.

Oliver, Edmund H. *The Country School in Non-English Speaking Communities in Saskatchewan.* Originally delivered as an address to the Saskatchewan Public Education League, Sept. 22, 1915, and subsequently published in pamphlet form. 18 pp.

    Oliver (1882-1935) was a lecturer in history at McMaster University from 1905 to 1909 when he became a professor of history and economics at the University of Saskatchewan. From 1914 until his death he served as principal of St. Andrew's College, Saskatoon. He was elected moderator of the United Church of Canada in 1932. As a writer Oliver published several books on the history of western Canada, the role of the church in its development, and various agencies in the education of the immigrant and his children.

    Source: MacMillan Dictionary of Canadian Biography, 562-63.

Presbyterian Church in Canada. *The Acts and Proceedings of the General Assembly of the Presbyterian Church in Canada.* 1898-1925.

Sherbinin, Michael A. *The Galicians Dwelling in Canada and their Origin.* Winnipeg, Manitoba Free Press Co., 1906. 12 pp. Originally presented as a paper to the Historical and Scientific Society of Manitoba, subsequently published as the Society's Transaction No. 71.

    Sherbinin, a Russian convert to Presbyterianism and graduate of

St. Petersburg University, initially served as a Presbyterian missionary among the Doukhobors at Rosthern, Saskatchewan. He was later engaged by Manitoba College as an instructor for young Ukrainians anxious to enter either the ministry or teaching profession. With Ivan Bodrug he compiled *Handbook of the Ruthenian Language (Galician) being also a Handbook of English for the Ruthenians*. Winnipeg, Canada Northwest Publishing Co., 1905.

Woodsworth, James S. *Strangers Within our Gates* or *Coming Canadians*. Toronto, Department of the Missionary Society of the Methodist Church, 1909. 331 pp.

Woodsworth (1874-1942) received his B.A. from the University of Manitoba in 1896 and his B.D. from Victoria University (Toronto) in 1900. He was ordained into the ministry of the Methodist Church in 1896 and spent several years in pastoral service, mostly in Winnipeg, where he developed an interest in social welfare work, which included Ukrainians. Woodsworth's second book, *My Neighbor: A Study of City Conditions: A Plea for Social Service* (Toronto, Missionary Society of the Methodist Church, 1911), was written from the viewpoint of a social worker, but stressed the idea of social responsibility without the emphasis on race, creed, or colour that was so prominent in *Strangers Within our Gates*. In 1919 he was implicated in the Winnipeg General Strike but charges of sedition were withdrawn. Elected Labour member of Parliament for North Winnipeg in 1921, he represented that constituency until his death. In 1932 Woodsworth became chairman of the national council of the Co-operative Commonwealth Federation (CCF) and the parliamentary leader of the new party.

Source: Macmillan Dictionary of Canadian Biography, 813.

Yeigh, Frank. *Through the Heart of Canada*. Toronto, Henry Frowde, 1911.

Yeigh (1861-1935) was educated in his native Ontario, where he was later employed in the civil service. In 1908 he left the civil service to become a lecturer, journalist, and social activist. *Through the Heart of Canada* was the product of a tour of the country. Ukrainians are discussed in chapter X, "The Foreigner in Canada" (176-92).

Source: Macmillan Dictionary of Canadian Biography, 817.

Articles

Chipman, George F. "Winnipeg: The Melting Pot," *Canadian Magazine of Politics, Science, Art and Literature,* Vol. XXXIII (1909), 412-16.

Chipman graduated from the Truro Normal School, Nova Scotia, in 1900, after which he taught for several years in rural Alberta among different nationalities.

Source: Provincial Archives of Alberta, Acc. 69.152.

d'Easum, Basil C. "A Galician Wedding," *Canadian Magazine of Politics, Science, Art and Literature,* Vol. XIII (1899), 83-84.

An Anglican minister, Geoffrey C. d'Easum, was a missionary in northern Alberta, a resident of Fort Saskatchewan, and a rural dean in Edmonton in the period under discussion. Basil C. d'Easum, undoubtedly related, was once justice of the peace in Fort Saskatchewan.

Source: Provincial Archives of Alberta, Information File.

Elston, Miriam. "The Canadian Slav and the War," *Graphic* (1917).

___ "English Schools for Foreigners in Alberta," *Westminster* (n.d., *circa* 1916), 425-32.

___ "A Greek Easter Service," *Onward* (April 22, 1916), 131.

___ "Making Ruthenians into Canadians: An Interesting Experiment in Education," *Graphic* (April 4, 1914).

___ "Meeting Needs on the Frontier: My Acquaintance with Lamont Hospital," *Onward* (n.d.).

___ "Our Little Russian Brother," *Christian Guardian* (1916). Reprinted in Gillese, J.P., editor-in-chief, *Chinook Arch: A Centennial Anthology of Alberta Writing.* (Edmonton, Queen's Printer, 1967), 46-54.

___ "The Russian in our Midst," *Westminster* (1915), 530-36.

___ "A Russian Wedding in Alberta," *East and West* (March 18, 1916), 93.

___ "A Ruthenian Day of Days: When the Albertan Colony, who ten years ago were known as 'Sifton's sheepskins,' Consecrated a Greek Church in the Name of Civilization," *Canadian Courier* (n.d.), 12-13. With minor changes, essentially the same article also appeared in the London *Graphic* as "The Ruthenian Invaders of Alberta."

Elston (1874-1974) came to Alberta from her native Ontario in 1908. She became noted as a journalist, particularly for her articles on the Ukrainian colony east of Edmonton, where she taught in the years prior to World War I. She planned to publish a book on Ukrainians but the paper shortage after 1914 forced her to abandon the project, although she continued to write abbreviated sketches based on her personal experiences. In the inter-war years she and her sister operated a millinery shop in Edmonton and until 1939 she taught millinery and dressmaking at the Edmonton Technical School. Copies of her articles on Ukrainians can be found in the Provincial Archives of Alberta (Acc. 65.55).

Source: Provincial Archives of Alberta, Acc. 65.55 and Information File.

Hardy, J.H. "The Ruthenians in Alberta," *Onward* (Nov. 1, 1913), 346-47.

It can be assumed from his article that Hardy was a school teacher among Ukrainians.

Murphy, Emily C. [Janey Canuck]. "Communing With Ruthenians," *Canadian Magazine of Politics, Science, Art and Literature,* Vol. XL (March 1913), 403-10. Essentially the same article appeared in

her *Seeds of Pine*. London, New York and Toronto, Hodder &
Stoughton, 1914, chapter XIX, 212-13.

Murphy (1868-1933) came to western Canada with her husband,
the Rev. Arthur Murphy, in 1904. An important figure in
philanthropic and humanitarian causes in Alberta, she was
appointed judge of the juvenile court in Edmonton and in 1925
became the official visitor of jails and mental hospitals in Alberta.
As Janey Canuck, she wrote several books, drawing primarily on
personal experiences. Her concern with Ukrainian Canadians was
not marked.

Source: *Macmillan Dictionary of Canadian Biography,* 539.

Woodsworth, J.S. "Nation Building," *University Magazine,* Vol. XIII
(February 1917), 85-99.

Unpublished Manuscripts

Woodsworth, James S., "Ukrainian Rural Communities," Report of
an Investigation by the Bureau of Social Research, Governments of
Manitoba, Saskatchewan and Alberta. Winnipeg, Jan. 25, 1917.
157 pp.

Government Records

Alberta. Department of Education. *Annual Reports* 1907-1916.
Edmonton, Government Printer, 1908-1917.

Canada. Department of the Interior. *Annual Reports* 1896-1906.
Ottawa, Queen's/King's Printer, 1897-1907.

Canada. House of Commons. *Official Record of the Debates* 1898-
1906. Ottawa, Queen's/King's Printer, 1898-1906.

Manitoba. Department of Education. *Annual Reports* 1896-1920.
Winnipeg, Government Printer, 1897-1921.

Saskatchewan. Department of Education. *Annual Reports* 1906-1920.
Regina, Government Printer, 1907-1921.

II. 1919 - 1945

Books and Pamphlets

Bryce, Peter H. *The Value to Canada of the Continental Immigrant.*
Ottawa, 1928. 56 pp.

Bryce attended the University of Toronto where he received the
Gold Medal in Science and graduated at the top of his class in
medical college. He also studied at the Royal College of Physicians
and Surgeons in Edinburgh. As secretary of the Provincial Board
of Health in Ontario, he expanded its public health service and was
responsible for drafting the Public Health Act of 1884. In 1904

Bryce went to Ottawa to organize the medical service of the federal Department of Immigration. He was its chief medical officer for nearly twenty years when the mass European immigration to Canada was at its peak. With legal assistance, Bryce drafted the 1906 Immigration Act. To him, Ukrainians were a valuable economic asset.

Catholic Truth Society of Canada. *Vindication of Bishop Budka: Full Record of Investigation: A String of Unfounded Charges: Judge Paterson's Summary.* Toronto, 1919. 6 pp.

Civil Liberties Association of Toronto. *An Appeal for Justice: The Case of the Seized Properties of the Ukrainian Labour-Farmer Temple Association.* Toronto, 34 pp.

Cormie, John A. *Canada and the New Canadians.* Toronto, Social Service Council of Canada, Dec., 1931. 30 pp.

At the time of writing, the Rev. J.A. Cormie was the Manitoba superintendent of home missions of the United Church of Canada.

Culbertson, Ely. *The Strange Lives of One Man: An Autobiography.* Chicago, Philadelphia, and Toronto, John C. Winston Co., 1940.

Culbertson claimed that his mother was the "daughter of a Cossack chief," which undoubtedly explains why, in spite of his American background, he was sympathetic to the Ukrainian labourers he encountered in Canada and willingly came to their defence.

England, Robert. *The Central European Immigrant in Canada.* Toronto, Macmillan, 1929. 238 pp.

___ *The Colonization of Western Canada: A Study of Contemporary Land Settlement (1896-1934).* London, P.S. King & Son, 1936. 341 pp.

Awarded a scholarship by the Province of Saskatchewan, England (1894-   ) pursued his studies of the assimilation problem at the College Libre des Sciences Sociales in Paris. He served for many years as the continental superintendent of the Colonization Department of the CNR and was attuned to the realities of immigration.

Foster, Kate A. *Our Canadian Mosaic.* Toronto, Dominion Council of the Y.W.C.A., 1926. 150 pp.

Gibbon, John Murray. *Canadian Mosaic: The Making of a Northern Nation.* Toronto, McClelland & Stewart, 1938. 455 pp.

Gibbon (1875-1952), educated at Oxford, worked as a journalist in London until 1907 when he was invited to supervise the European publicity work of the CPR. In 1913 he emigrated to Canada to become general publicity agent for the railway, holding this position until his retirement in 1945. Organizer of the New Canadian folk festivals across Canada and publisher of numerous articles on the folk heritages of Canadians, Gibbon also translated and adapted folk songs to the Canadian environment. *Canadian Mosaic* received the Governor-General's Award. Gibbon was the founder and first president of the Canadian Authors' Association and in 1922 was elected a fellow of the Royal Society of Canada.

Frances Swyripa

Source: *Macmillan Dictionary of Canadian Biography*, 263.

Grocholski, J.S.W., ed. *Preliminary Survey on Integration of the Canadian Racial, Cultural and Nationality Groups from the Standpoint of Canadians of Various Origins other than British or French*. Private printing, limited edition. Toronto, Canadians All Research Division, 1944. 31 pp.

Hayward, Victoria. *Romantic Canada*. Toronto, Macmillan, 1922.

Romantic Canada was the result of a journey across Canada by Hayward and another American, Edith Watson. John Gibbon has credited Hayward with the first use of the term "mosaic." References to Ukrainians were fleeting but they contributed to the author's picturesque and visionary view of Canada and her future.

Hunchak, Nicholas J. *Canadians of Ukrainian Origin: Population*. Winnipeg, Ukrainian Canadian Committee, 1945. 164 pp.

Hunchak was a graduate of the University of Saskatchewan (B.Sc., B.Acc.) and at the time of writing was employed in Winnipeg as an accountant.

Hunter, Alexander J. *A Friendly Adventure: The Story of the United Church Mission Among New Canadians at Teulon, Manitoba*. Toronto, Board of Home Missions of the United Church of Canada, 1929. 132 pp.

Hunter (1868-1940), M.D., D.D., arrived in Winnipeg in 1902 to serve with the Home Mission Committee of the Presbyterian Church in Canada. He was sent to Teulon, Manitoba, where he established a mission which was later expanded to include a hospital and boys' and girls' residential schools. He remained for many years, becoming intensely interested in the heritage of the Ukrainian people. Hunter was awarded the Order of the British Empire for his work among the Ukrainians in Canada.

Hutchison, Bruce. *The Unknown Country: Canada and her People*. New York, Coward-McCann, 1942.

A Canadian journalist, Hutchison's image of the Ukrainians was essentially descriptive and did not go beyond that of the peasant stereotype. He revealed a point of view that was a curious mixture of assimilation and the "mosaic" in his chapter "The Men in Sheepskin Coats" (272-88).

Kennedy, Howard A. *The Book of the West*. Toronto, Ryerson Press, 1925.

Kirkconnell, Watson. *Canada, Europe, and Hitler*. Toronto, Oxford University Press, 1939. 213 pp.

___ *Canadian Overtones*. Winnipeg, Columbia Press, Ltd., 1935. 104 pp.

___ *Canadians All: A Primer of Canadian National Unity*. Ottawa, Issued by the Director of Public Information under the authority of the Minister of National War Services, June, 1941. 48 pp.

___ *Our Communists and the New Canadians*. Originally delivered as an address before a meeting of the Canadian Club in Toronto, Feb. 1, 1943, and later published in pamphlet form. 24 pp.

___ *Our Ukrainian Loyalists: The Ukrainian Canadian Committee*.

Winnipeg, Ukrainian Canadian Committee, 1943. 28 pp.
___ *The Ukrainian Canadians and the War*. Toronto, Oxford University Press, 1940. 30 pp.

Kirkconnell (1895-1977) received his education at Queen's University and Oxford. He taught English and classics at Wesley College, Winnipeg, and from 1940 to 1948 he was head of the English Department at McMaster University until he became president of Acadia University. He retired in 1963. During World War I he was an officer of the federal Department of Justice, responsible for interned aliens. Kirkconnell was elected to the Royal Society of Canada in 1936 and was awarded the Lorne Pierce Medal for his outstanding contribution to Canadian literature. A noted linguist and scholar, he included the history and literature of the Ukrainian Canadians among his interests and literary pursuits. With C.H. Andrusyshen he translated two voluminous works, *The Poetical Works of Taras Shevchenko* (1963) and *The Ukrainian Poets* (1963).
Source: Nora Story, *Oxford Companion to Canadian History and Literature* (Toronto, Oxford University Press, 1967), 406.

McClung, Nellie L. *The Stream Runs Fast: My Own Story*. Toronto, Thomas Allen, Ltd., 1945. Chap. XIX: "New Places and New People," 153-69.

McClung (1873-1951) was a well-known champion of women's rights and from 1921 to 1926 sat as a Liberal member of the Alberta Legislature. She had numerous publications to her credit, of which *The Stream Runs Fast* was a sequel to an earlier autobiographical work, *Clearing in the West*. In *The Stream Runs Fast* she described the work of the Methodist mission among the Ukrainians at Pakan, Alberta.
Source: Macmillan Dictionary of Canadian Biography, 432.

Methodius, Brother S. *Canadians on the March*. Incorporating the first in a series of radio broadcasts over CJGX entitled, "Canada United." Yorkton, Ukrainian Canadian Cultural Group, 1944. 52 pp.

Brother Methodius (born Basil Koziak, 1904) was the first Ukrainian Greek Catholic to become a Brother of the Christian Schools (F.S.C.) with permission to retain his Eastern rite. President of the Ukrainian Canadian Cultural Group of Yorkton, he has also served as director of the Taras Shevchenko Institute, Edmonton, St. Joseph's College, Yorkton, and the Sheptytsky Institute in Saskatoon. He possessed an M.A. from the University of Toronto and was instrumental in securing Ukrainian as an accredited course in Saskatchewan high schools.
Source: Joseph M. Lazarenko, editor-in-chief, *The Ukrainian Pioneers in Alberta, Canada*. (Edmonton, Alberta Printing Company for the Ukrainian Pioneers Association in Edmonton, 1970), 274.

Paluk, William. *Canadian Cossacks: Essays, Articles and Stories on Ukrainian Canadian Life*. Winnipeg, Canadian Ukrainian Review Publishing Co., 1943. 130 pp.

Paluk (1914-   ), born and educated in Winnipeg, received his
B.A. from United College in 1936. A contributing editor to the
Canadian Ukrainian Review, he was also well-known as a director
of Ukrainian choirs.

Scott, W.L. *The Ukrainians: Our Most Pressing Problem.* Toronto,
Catholic Truth Society of Canada, 1931. 64 pp.

A Catholic in good standing, W.L. Scott wrote his pamphlet to
arouse Canadian Catholics to the defence of Ukrainian-Canadian
Catholics who were being encouraged to convert to other faiths,
and to make them aware of the unique religious background of
Ukrainian Greek Catholicism.

Shohan, Rudolf [Raymond A. Davies]. *This is Our Land: Ukrainian
Canadians Against Hitler.* Toronto, Progress Books, 1943. 158 pp.

A left-wing journalist and author during World War II, Shohan
(1908-   ), using the Davies pseudonym, has published from a
communist point of view, while importing and exporting Soviet
and East European publications.

Sisler, William J. *Peaceful Invasion.* Winnipeg, Ketchen Printing Co.,
1944. 126 pp.

Long a teacher and school principal among 'New Canadians' —
mostly in metropolitan Winnipeg — Sisler discussed the problems
of assimilation in an urban environment. The Sisler collection in
the Public Archives of Manitoba contains numerous manuscripts
and photographs on the development and progress of Ukrainian
Canadians depicting conditions in rural Manitoba.

Smith, William G. *Building the Nation: The Churches' Relation to the
Immigrant.* Toronto, Ryerson Press, 1922. 202 pp.

___ *A Study in Canadian Immigration.* Toronto, Ryerson Press,
1920. 406 pp.

Smith (1872-1943), educationalist and author, received his B.A.
in 1899 from Victoria College (Toronto). Following employment as
a professor of sociology at the University of Toronto, he became
the director of the School of Social Work at the University of
Manitoba. *Building the Nation* was written to aid home
missionaries and was published for three Protestant
denominations; the immigration study was written for the
Canadian National Committee for Mental Hygiene.

Source: Macmillan Dictionary of Canadian Biography, 703.

Ukrainian National Federation of Canada. *A Program and a Record.*
Winnipeg and Saskatoon, March 1943. 32 pp.

Young, Charles H. *The Ukrainian Canadians: A Study in Assimilation.* Toronto, Thomas Nelson & Sons, Ltd., 1931. 327 pp.

Articles

Baumgartner, F.W. "Central European Immigration," *Queen's
Quarterly,* Vol. XXXVII (Winter 1930), 183-92.

As a staff member of the European Immigration Service of the
CNR, Baumgartner had travelled extensively in central Europe.

Chicanot, Eugene L. "Homesteading the Citizen: Canadian Festivals Promote Cultural Exchange," *Commonwealth,* Vol. X (May 1929), 94-95.

___ "Moulding a Nation," *Dalhousie Review,* Vol. IX (1929), 232-37.

Elston, Miriam. "Our Own Slav Problem: Ukrainians in Canada," *Graphic* (Aug. 9, 1919).

___ "Ruthenians in Western Canada. I. Public Schools," *Onward* (April 12, 1919).

___ "Ruthenians in Western Canada. II. School Teaching Amongst the Russians," *Onward* (April 19, 1919).

___ "Ruthenians in Western Canada. III. Canadian Citizens from Russians," *Onward* (April 26, 1919).

___ "Ruthenians in Western Canada. IV. When Sickness Visits A Russian Home," *Onward* (May 3, 1919).

Gibbon, John Murray. "The Foreign Born," *Queen's Quarterly,* Vol. XXVII (April 1920), 331-51.

___ "European Seeds in the Canadian Garden," *Transactions of the Royal Society of Canada,* Vol. XVII, 3rd series, 1923, sec. ii, (May 1923), 119-29.

___ "A Secular Bible for a New Canada," *Transactions of the Royal Society of Canada,* Vol. XXXVI, 3rd series, 1942, sec. ii, (May 1942), 93-100.

Hamilton, Louis. "Foreigners in the Canadian West," *Dalhousie Review,* Vol. XVII (1938), 448-60.

Heap, F. "Ukrainians in Canada: An Estimate of the Presence, Ideals, Religion, Tendencies, and Citizenship of Perhaps Three Hundred Thousand Ukrainians in Canada," *Canadian Magazine of Politics, Science, Art and Literature,* Vol. LIII (1919), 39-44.

Kirkconnell, W. "The European Canadians in their Press," *Canadian Historical Association Report* (1940), 85-92.

Koohtow, P.W. "Ukrainian Theatre in Canada," *Canadian Forum,* Vol. X (July 1930), 386.

Lower, A.R.M. "Motherlands," *Dalhousie Review,* Vol. XVIII (1938), 143-48.

    Lower (1889-   ), a Canadian social historian, has expressed very definite views on the doubtful value of immigration to Canada, and has criticized the "mosaic" concept of Canadian identity.

Murray, Walter. "Continental Europeans in Western Canada," *Queen's Quarterly,* Vol. XXXVIII (Winter 1931), 63-75.

    Murray (1866-1945) obtained his B.A. from the University of New Brunswick in 1886 and his M.D. from Edinburgh University in 1891. He also studied in Berlin. A professor of philosophy at the University of New Brunswick and at Dalhousie University, he served as president of the University of Saskatchewan from 1908 to 1937 and was generally sympathetic towards Ukrainian aspirations. He was elected a fellow of the Royal Society of Canada in 1918. *Source: Macmillan Dictionary of Canadian Biography,* 542.

Frances Swyripa

Reaman, George E. "Canadianization of the Foreign-Born," *Canadian Magazine of Politics, Science, Art and Literature,* Vol. LIX (Oct. 1922), 445-50.

Ridout, Denzil G. "European Sources of Non-Anglo-Saxons in Canada," *Canadian Geographical Journal,* Vol. II (March 1931), 201-23.

The Rev. D.G. Ridout was the assistant secretary of the Missionary Maintenance Fund of the United Church of Canada, and in that capacity not only studied the life of the non-Anglo-Saxon people in Canada but also travelled to their European homelands to obtain personal impressions and observations.

Scott, W.L. "The Privy Council and Greek Catholics," *Canadian Law Times* (April 1919), 1-7.

Simpson, George W. "The Blending of Traditions in Western Canadian Settlement," *Canadian Historical Association Report* (1944), 46-52.

Simpson was for many years the head of the Department of History at the University of Saskatchewan, a noted specialist in the history of the Slavic peoples in Europe and America. In 1941 he published an *Historic Atlas of the Ukraine* and subsequently wrote and spoke about Ukrainian history. In 1939 he edited the English translation of Dmytro Doroshenko's *History of the Ukraine.* He was very active in the formation of the Ukrainian Canadian Committee.

Wright, J.F.C. "Ukrainian-Canadians," *Canadian Geographical Journal,* Vol. XXV (Aug. 1942), 74-87.

Yeigh, Frank. "New Canadians Making Good," *Canadian Magazine of Politics, Science, Art and Literature,* Vol. LIX (July 1922), 227-35.

Younge, Eva R. "Population Movements and the Assimilation of Alien Groups in Canada," *Canadian Journal of Economics and Political Science,* Vol. X (Aug. 1944), 372-80.

Theses and Unpublished Manuscripts

Bayley, Charles M. "The Social Structure of the Italian and Ukrainian Immigrant Communities in Montreal, 1935-1937." Unpublished M.A. thesis, McGill University, 1939. 292 pp.

Bercuson, Leonard. "Education in the Bloc Settlements of Western Canada." Unpublished M.A. thesis, McGill University, 1941. 270 pp.

Byrne, Timothy C. "The Ukrainian Community in North Central Alberta." Unpublished M.A. thesis, University of Alberta, 1937. 100 pp.

Byrne received his B.A. in 1932, M.A. in 1937, and B.Ed. in 1942, all from the University of Alberta. He was granted his D.Ed. from the University of Colorado in 1956. Successively a teacher, superintendent of schools, a high school inspector, and the chief superintendent of schools for Alberta, Byrne became the province's deputy minister of education in 1966. He resigned in 1971 to assume the presidency of Athabasca University.

Deverell, Jessie M. "The Ukrainian Teacher as an Agent of Cultural Assimilation." Unpublished M.A. thesis, University of Toronto, 1941. 114 pp.

Hunter, Alexander J. "The Ukrainians: Their Historical and Cultural Background." Paper presented to the Historical and Scientific Society of Manitoba, Jan. 13, 1932. 26 pp. Published in part in series III (10), 1955, of the *Transactions of the Historical and Scientific Society of Manitoba.*

Mamchur, Stephen W. "The Economic and Social Adjustment of Slavic Immigrants in Canada: With Special Reference to the Ukrainians in Montreal." Unpublished M.A. thesis, McGill University, 1934. 302 pp.

McAllister, John W. "The Rural School as a Community Centre: A Discussion Dealing With the Problem of the Assimilation of New Canadians in Western Canada." Unpublished M.Sc. thesis, University of Alberta, 1925. 70 pp.

Robinson, Claude H. "A Study of the Written Language Errors of 1238 Pupils of Ukrainian Origin." Unpublished B.Ed. thesis, University of Alberta, 1934. 58 pp.

Woollatt, Lorne H. "A Study to Discover any Characteristic Differences in Sentence Structure in the Written English of Saskatchewan Elementary School Pupils Belonging to Different National Groups." Unpublished M.Ed. thesis, University of Saskatchewan, 1944. 89 pp.

III. 1946 - 1970

Books and Pamphlets

Association of United Ukrainian Canadians and the Workers' Benevolent Association of Canada. *Tribute to our Ukrainian Pioneers in Canada's First Century.* Proceedings of a Special Convention. March 23, 1966. 100 pp.

Darcovich, William. *Ukrainians in Canada: The Struggle to Retain their Identity.* Ottawa, Ukrainian Self-Reliance Association, Ottawa Branch, 1967. 38 pp.

Davidson, Gordon A. *Ukrainians in Canada: A Study in Canadian Immigration.* Originally delivered as an address to the McGill University Historical Club, Nov. 30, 1944, and published in pamphlet form in 1947. 23 pp.

Fry, Olivia R. *My Heritage from the Builders of Canada.* New York, Carleton Press, 1967. 183 pp.

Fry (nee Yakimchuk) was a left-leaning second-generation Ukrainian Canadian, who founded the Vancouver (Kingcrest) Business and Professional Women's Club.

Gibbon, John M. *New Color for the Canadian Mosaic: The Displaced Persons.* Toronto, McClelland & Stewart, 1951. 30 pp.

Kaye, Vladimir J. *Early Ukrainian Settlements in Canada 1895-1900: Dr. Josef Oleskow's Role in the Settlement of the Canadian Northwest.* Toronto, University of Toronto Press (for the Ukrainian Canadian Research Foundation), 1964. 420 pp.

___ *Slavic Groups in Canada.* Winnipeg, Ukrainian Free Academy of Sciences, Slavistica #12, 1951. 30 pp.

Kaye-Kysilewsky (1896-1976) was born into a distinguished Ukrainian family. Educated at the University of Vienna and the Institute of Eastern European Studies, where he received his Ph.D. in 1924, he emigrated to Canada, and from 1928 to 1930 edited *Zakhidni Visti (Western News)* in Edmonton. He returned to England for post-graduate studies at the School of Slavonic and East European Studies at the University of London. While director of the Ukrainian Press Bureau in London, he was also a member of the Royal Institute of International Affairs. Back in Canada in 1940, Kaye became connected with an information branch in the Department of National War Services designed to promote co-operation among Canadians of non-British and non-French origin, acting as a liaison officer with the various ethnic groups and their publications. In 1950 he was appointed associate professor at the University of Ottawa, specializing in the migration, ethnology, and the settlement of Slavic groups in Canada. His meticulous research on Ukrainian Canadians has been of great significance.

Source: Foreword by G.W. Simpson, *Early Ukrainian Settlements in Canada,* vii-x.

Kiriak, Illia. *Sons of the Soil.* Translated by Michael Luchkovich. Toronto, Ryerson Press, 1959. 303 pp.

Kiriak (1888-1955) emigrated to Canada from Ukraine in 1907 and after receiving his education at the Mohyla Institute in Saskatoon, he taught for several years in Alberta. Although he also wrote short stories and poetry, *Sons of the Soil* was his major work.

Source: Volodymyr Kubijovic, ed., *Entsyklopediia Ukrainoznavstva* (Ukrainian Encyclopedia), Vol. II, pt. 3 (1959), 1033.

Lazarenko, Joseph M., ed. *The Ukrainian Pioneers in Alberta, Canada.* Edmonton, Alberta Printing Company (for the Ukrainian Pioneers Association), 1970. 384 pp.

Lewenec-Kohuska, Natalia. *Forty Years in Retrospect.* Translated by Sonia Cipywnyk. Winnipeg, Ukrainian Women's Association of Canada, 1967. 32 pp.

Luchkovich, Michael. *A Ukrainian Canadian in Parliament: Memoirs of Michael Luchkovich.* Toronto, Ukrainian Canadian Research Foundation, 1965. 128 pp.

American-born Michael Luchkovich (1892-1973) came to Canada in 1907, enrolled at Manitoba College, and in 1912 obtained his first teaching position in rural Alberta. In 1926 he was elected member of Parliament for the Vegreville constituency as a

representative of the United Farmers of Alberta. He held his seat until 1935, representing Canada at the International Inter-Parliamentary Union Congress held in Romania in 1931. In his later years he translated Kiriak's *Sons of the Soil* and Nicholas Prychodko's *One of the Fifteen Million.*
Source: Entsyklopediia ukrainoznavstva, Vol. II, pt. 4 (1962), 1390.

Lysenko, Vera. *Men in Sheepskin Coats: A Study in Assimilation.* Toronto, Ryerson Press, 1947. 312 pp.

___ *Yellow Boots.* Toronto, Ryerson Press, 1954. 314 pp.
Canadian-born Vera Lysenko was a Winnipeg school teacher and left-wing journalist.

MacGregor, James G. *Vilni Zemli/ Free Lands: The Ukrainian Settlement of Alberta.* Toronto, McClelland and Stewart, 1969. 274 pp.
A popular historian with numerous publications to his credit, MacGregor (1905-   ) has written no additional work on the Ukrainian Canadians. In 1968 *Vilni Zemli* was awarded the Beaver Award by the Edmonton Branch of the Hudson's Bay Company. Trained as an electrical engineer at the University of Alberta (B.Sc. 1929), he was employed for many years by Canadian Utilities Limited before resigning in 1952 to become chairman of the Alberta Power Commission. In 1956 he was appointed chairman of the Royal Commission on the Development of Northern Alberta.

Mandryka, M.I. *History of Ukrainian Literature in Canada.* Winnipeg, Ukrainian Free Academy of Sciences, 1968. 274 pp.
Mandryka (1886-   ) emigrated to Canada in 1928 after receiving his education in Kiev, Sofia, and Prague (where he obtained an LL.D.). A noted poet, he has continued to publish in Canada.

Marunchak, Michael H. *The Ukrainian Canadians: A History.* Winnipeg, Ukrainian Free Academy of Sciences, 1970. 792 pp.
Michael H. Marunchak (1914-   ) was educated at the University of Lviv and the Ukrainian Free University in Prague, receiving an LL.D. in 1941. He came to Canada after World War II as part of the movement of displaced persons. His interest in Ukrainian-Canadian history has resulted in numerous studies, published almost exclusively in the Ukrainian language.

Methodius, Brother S. *Reverend Brother Stanislaus Joseph, F.S.C.* Yorkton, St. Joseph's College, 1953. 30 pp.

Oakburn Centennial Committee. *Echoes: Oakburn, Manitoba, 1870-1970,* Oakburn, 1970. 118 pp.

Romaniuk, Gus. *Taking Root in Canada: An Autobiography.* Winnipeg, Columbia Press, Ltd., 1954. 283 pp.
Romaniuk arrived in Canada as a child in 1912 and pursued a varied career at Riverton, Manitoba, where the marginal lands settled by his father proved unsuitable for cultivation.

Semczuk, Rev. Stepan. *Centennial of Canada and 75 Years of Ukrainian Catholic Church.* Winnipeg, 1967. 7 pp.

Frances Swyripa

Fr. Semczuk (1899-　) is a priest in the Ukrainian Greek
Catholic Church of Canada, a founder of the Ukrainian Catholic
Brotherhood (a lay organization), and a Ukrainian-language poet.
Ukrainian Canadian Committee. *On Language and Culture.* Win-
nipeg, 1962. 10 pp.
Ukrainian Professional and Business Men's Club. *25th Anniversary
Review, 1943-1968.* Winnipeg, 1968. 149 pp.
Woycenko, Olha. *Canada's Cultural Heritage: Ukrainian Contribu-
tion.* Originally delivered as an address to a symposium on
Canada's Cultural Heritage at the annual meeting of the Provincial
Council of Women, Winnipeg, Nov. 14-15, 1963. Winnipeg,
Ukrainian Free Academy of Sciences. Litopys #22, 1964. 16 pp.
—— *The Ukrainians in Canada.* Winnipeg, Trident Press, 1967. 271
pp.
Woycenko (1909-　) has been an energetic researcher into
Ukrainian-Canadian development with numerous publications (in
both English and Ukrainian) to her credit. Her most ambitious
undertaking has been a series, *Litopys ukraiinskoho zhyttia v
Kanadi* (Annals of Ukrainian Life in Canada), consisting of
selected excerpts from the newspaper *Ukrainskyi holos* (*Ukrainian
Voice*) covering all aspects of Ukrainian-Canadian life. Woycenko
has also been highly active in Ukrainian women's organizations
and served as president of the Ukrainian Canadian Women's
Association from 1948 to 1954.
Source: Entsyklopediia ukrainoznavstva, Vol. II, pt. 1 (1959),
302.
Yuzyk, Paul. *The Ukrainian Canadians: Their Place and Role in
Canadian Life.* Toronto, Ukrainian Canadian Business and
Professional Federation, 1967. 104 pp.
—— *The Ukrainians in Manitoba: A Social History.* Toronto,
University of Toronto Press (under the auspices of the Historical
and Scientific Society of Manitoba), 1953. 232 pp.
Saskatchewan-born Paul Yuzyk (1913-　) received his M.A.
from the University of Saskatchewan in 1948 and his Ph.D. from
the University of Minnesota in 1958. For several years on the
teaching staff of the University of Manitoba (Departments of
History and Slavic Studies), he was later associated with the
University of Ottawa. Appointed to the Canadian Senate in 1963,
Yuzyk has been a prominent spokesman for multiculturalism in
Canada.

Articles

Boudreau, Joseph A. "Western Canada's 'Enemy Aliens' in World War
One," *Alberta Historical Review,* Vol. 12 (Winter 1964), 1-9.
Chalmers, John W. "Strangers in our Midst," *Alberta Historical
Review,* Vol. 16 (Winter 1968), 18-23.
Chomiak, M. "Contribution of Ukrainians to the Development and
Growth of Schools in Alberta," *Slavs in Canada,* Vol. II (1968),
273-77.

Francis, Anne. "Canada's Slavic Seasoning," *Geographical Magazine,* Vol. XXVI (1953), 84-88.

Francis was for some time a news commentator for the CBC and a resident of Winnipeg, which gave her the opportunity to obtain a first-hand knowledge of Ukrainian Canadians.

Gibbon, John M. "Folk-song and Feudalism," *Transactions of the Royal Society of Canada,* Vol. XLII, 3rd series, 1948, sec. ii (May, 1948), 73-84.

Hobart, Charles W. "Adjustment of Ukrainians in Alberta: Alienation and Integration," *Slavs in Canada,* Vol. I (1966), 69-85.

Janishewskyj, W. "Ukrainian Engineers in Ontario," *Slavs in Canada,* Vol. II (1968), 168-77.

Kalbach, Warren E. "Some Demographic Aspects of Ukrainian Population in Canada," *Slavs in Canada,* Vol. I (1966), 54-68.

Kaye, V.J. "Early Ukrainian Graduates of Agricultural Colleges," *Slavs in Canada,* Vol. II (1968), 263-72.

___ "Three Phases of Ukrainian Immigration," *Slavs in Canada,* Vol. I (1966), 36-43.

___ "The Ukrainians in Canada," in J. Kosa (ed.), *Immigrants in Canada.* (Montreal, 1955), 12-16.

Kirkconnell, Watson. "Leviathan, Behemoth, Kraken," *Transactions of the Royal Society of Canada,* Vol. VI, 4th series, 1968, sec. ii, 161-70.

Lazarowich, Peter J. "Ukrainian Pioneers in Western Canada," *Alberta Historical Review,* Vol. V (Autumn 1957), 17-27.

Maslanyk, A., and M. Chomiak. "The Scientific Contribution of Ukrainians to the Industrial Development of Canada," *Slavs in Canada,* Vol. II (1968), 178-88.

Navalkowski, Anna. "Shandro School." *Alberta Historical Review,* Vol. XVIII (Autumn 1970), 8-14.

Navalkowski, the daughter of William N. Shandro, was one of the first pupils to attend Shandro School.

Nebel, Mabel R. "Rev. Thomas Johnson and the Insinger Experiment," *Saskatchewan History,* Vol. XI (1958), 1-16.

Nebel was a school teacher at the Presbyterian mission among Ukrainians at Insinger, Saskatchewan, for four summers.

Patterson, Sheila. "This New Canada: A Study of Changing People," *Queen's Quarterly,* Vol. LXII (Spring 1955), 80-88.

Pawliw, Orest. "Studies in Ukrainian Literature in Canada," *Slavs in Canada,* Vol. II (1968), 235-46.

Plawiuk, Mykola. "Ukrainian Credit Unions in Canada," *Slavs in Canada,* Vol. II (1968), 146-53.

Pobihushchy, Sidney I. "The Development of Political Socialization of Ukrainians in Alberta," *Slavs in Canada,* Vol. II (1968), 20-30.

Pohorecky, Zenon S., and A. Royick. "Anglicization of Ukrainian in Canada Between 1895 and 1970: A Case Study of Linguistic Crystallization," *Canadian Ethnic Studies Bulletin of the Research Centre for Canadian Ethnic Studies,* Vol. I (1969), 141-219.

Ponich, M.H. "Wasyl Eleniak: Father of Ukrainian Settlers in

163

Frances Swyripa

Canada," *Alberta Historical Review,* Vol. IV (Summer 1956), 17-18.

Ponich (1905-1957), an Alberta lawyer, was a Social Credit MLA from the predominantly Ukrainian Willingdon constituency from 1944 to 1955.

Royick, Alexander. "Ukrainian Settlements in Alberta," *Canadian Slavonic Papers,* Vol. X (1968), 278-97.

Rudnyckyj, Jaroslav B. "Ukrainian Free Academy of Science — UVAN of Canada." *Slavs in Canada,* Vol. II (1968), 207-11.

Rudnyckyj (1910-   ) received his Ph.D. from Lviv University in 1937. Since his immigration to Canada after World War II, he has published extensively on Ukrainian and Canadian topics. A noted philologist, he headed the Department of Slavic Studies at the University of Manitoba for many years and was a moving force behind the Ukrainian Free Academy of Sciences. He was also a member of the Royal Commission on Bilingualism and Biculturalism.

Source: Entsyklopediia ukrainoznavstva, Pt. 33 (1975), 2632.

Simpson, George W. "Father Delaere, Pioneer Missionary and Founder of Churches," *Saskatchewan History,* Vol. III (Winter 1950), 1-16.

Syrnick, John H. "Community Builders: Early Ukrainian Teachers," *Transactions of the Historical and Scientific Society of Manitoba,* series III (21), 1964-65, 25-34.

___ "The Ukrainian Canadian Committee: Its Significance in the Canadian Society," *Slavs in Canada,* Vol. II (1968), 67-77.

Toombs, M.P. "A Saskatchewan Experiment in Teacher Education, 1907-1917," *Saskatchewan History,* Vol. XVII (1964), 1-11.

Wangenheim, Elizabeth D. "Problems of Research on Ukrainians in Eastern Canada," *Slavs in Canada,* Vol. I (1966), 44-53.

___ "The Ukrainians: A Case Study of the 'Third Force'" in Peter Russell (ed.). *Nationalism in Canada.* Toronto, McGraw-Hill Co., 1966. 72-91.

Waggenheim has studied sociology at Waterloo Lutheran University and the Ontario Institute for Studies in Education.

Yuzyk, Paul. "The First Ukrainians in Manitoba," *Transactions of the Historical and Scientific Society of Manitoba,* series III, (8), 1953, 30-39.

Zuk, Radoslav. "Ukrainian Church Architecture in Canada," *Slavs in Canada,* Vol. II (1968), 229-34.

Radoslav Zuk is a noted architect of Ukrainian churches in North America. He received a B.Arch. from McGill University in 1956 and a M.Arch. from the Massachusetts Institute of Technology in 1960. He was an assistant professor of architecture at the University of Manitoba from 1960 to 1966, in which year he joined the staff of McGill University.

Theses and Unpublished Manuscripts

164   Cipywnyk, Sonia V. "Educational Implications of Ukrainian-English

Childhood Bilingualism in Saskatchewan." Unpublished M.Ed. thesis, University of Saskatchewan, 1968. 402 pp.

Foster, Matthew J. "Ethnic Settlement in the Barton Street Region of Hamilton, 1921-1961." Unpublished M.A. thesis, McMaster University, 1965. 236 pp.

Fromson, Ronald D. "Acculturation or Assimilation: A Geographical Analysis of Residential Segregation of Selected Ethnic Groups: Metropolitan Winnipeg 1951-1961." Unpublished M.A. thesis, University of Manitoba, 1965.

Harasym, Caroline Rose. "Cultural Orientation of Rural Ukrainian High School Students." Unpublished M.Ed. thesis, University of Calgary, 1969. 128 pp.

Piniuta, Harry. "The Organizational Life of Ukrainian Canadians; with Special Reference to the Ukrainian Canadian Committee." Unpublished M.A. thesis, University of Ottawa, 1952. 137 pp.

Royick, Alexander. "Lexical Borrowings in Alberta Ukrainian." Unpublished M.A. thesis, University of Alberta, 1965. 118 pp.

Saruk, Alec. "Academic Performance of Students of Ukrainian Descent and the Cultural Orientation of their Parents." Unpublished M.Ed. thesis, University of Alberta, 1966. 107 pp.

Skuba, Michael. "An Analysis of English Errors and Difficulties Among Grade Ten Students in the Smoky Lake School Division." Unpublished M.Ed. thesis, University of Alberta, 1955. 106 pp.

Skwarok, John. "The Ukrainian Settlers in Canada and their Schools, with Reference to Government, French-Canadian, and Ukrainian Missionary Influences, 1891-1921." M.Ed. thesis, University of Alberta, 1958. Published by Basilian Press in Edmonton, 1958. 157 pp.
    The Rev. J. Skwarok (1918-   ) was ordained a priest in the Order of St. Basil the Great in 1947.

Stefanow, Marlene. "A Study of Intermarriage of Ukrainians in Saskatchewan." Unpublished M.A. thesis, University of Saskatchewan, 1962. 112 pp.

Sullivan, David M. "An Investigation of the English Disabilities of Ukrainian and Polish Students in Grades IX, X, XI, XII of Alberta." Unpublished M.Ed. thesis, University of Alberta, 1946. 104 pp.

Trosky, Odarka S. "A Historical Study of the Development of the Ukrainian Greek Orthodox Church of Canada and its Role in the Field of Education (1918-1964)." M.Ed. thesis, University of Manitoba, 1965. Published by the author in Winnipeg in 1968 as *The Ukrainian Greek Orthodox Church in Canada.* 87 pp.
    Trosky (nee Hrycyna) attended Manitoba Normal School and subsequently taught in Greater Winnipeg for fourteen years. In 1965 she was appointed assistant professor in the Faculty of Education at the University of Manitoba. She has also served as a member of the Curriculum Committee in Language Arts for the Manitoba Department of Education.

Ukrainian Canadian Committee. "Brief Presented to the Right

Honourable Vincent Massey, P.C., C-H, Chairman and Members of the Royal Commission on National Development in the Arts, Letters and Sciences." Winnipeg, Oct. 13, 1949. 14 pp.

Veryha, Wasyl. "The Ukrainian Canadian Committee: Its Origin and War Activity." Unpublished M.A. thesis, University of Ottawa, 1967. 160 pp.

Wenstob, Murray. "The Work of the Methodist Church among Settlers in Alberta up to 1914, with Special Reference to the Formation of Congregations and Work among the Ukrainian People." Unpublished B.D. thesis, University of Alberta, 1959. 130 pp.

Woycenko, Olha. "Ukrainian Contribution to Canada's Cultural Life. Report Presented to the Royal Commission on Bilingualism and Biculturalism." Winnipeg, Oct. 1965. 116 pp.

Yuzyk, Paul. "The History of the Ukrainian Greek Catholic (Uniate) Church in Canada." Unpublished M.A. thesis, University of Saskatchewan, 1948. 250 pp.

___ "Ukrainian Greek Orthodox Church of Canada (1918-1951)." Unpublished Ph.D. dissertation, University of Minnesota, 1958. 334 pp.

Zborowsky, Walter I. "Ukrainian Culture: A Study of Ukrainian Cultural Patterns and their Implications in the Social Casework Process." Unpublished M.S.W. thesis, University of Ottawa, 1955. 69 pp.

Government Publications

Report of the Royal Commission on Bilingualism and Biculturalism. Book IV: *The Cultural Contribution of the Other Ethnic Groups.* Ottawa, Queen's Printer, 1970. 352 pp.

Index

167

168

Index